GLOBAL
LEARNING
STRATEGIES

Accelerated Distance Learning

*THE NEW WAY TO EARN YOUR COLLEGE DEGREE
IN THE TWENTY-FIRST CENTURY*

by Brad Voeller

Published by Dedicated Publishing
18212 Hwy 46 W, Spring Branch, TX 78070

Printed in USA

Design by Pioneer Design Group

THIRD EDITION
ISBN 0-9701563-1-6

About Global Learning Strategies

Global Learning Strategies is a division of the Global Leadership Institute, Inc., a nonprofit institution dedicated to developing effective and innovative leadership.

Recognizing the increasing expense and lack of efficiency in the traditional model of higher education, the mission of Global Learning Strategies is to advance the understanding, practice, and development of Accelerated Distance Learning for the benefit of students worldwide.

Global Learning Strategies conducts research, produces publications, and provides educational programs to assist students in achieving their educational goals.

*For more information about Global Learning Strategies,
e-mail info@GlobalLearningStrategies.org,
or visit www.GlobalLearningStrategies.org.*

Contents

INTRODUCTION ix

PART I: BLAZING A NEW TRAIL 1

1. The Paradigm Shift: *Why Accelerated Distance Learning*
   Is THE Educational Strategy for the Information Age. 5

2. The Traps of Traditional Education:
   What They Are and How to Avoid Them 11

PART II: DISTANCE LEARNING 17

3. Credit-by-Examination:
   The Best-Kept Secret in Higher Education 21

4. Portfolio Assessment:
   Credit for Real-Life Learning. 35

5. Internships:
   College Credits That Will Jump-Start Your Career 47

6. Taking Online and Correspondence Courses:
   College Classes Beyond the Four Walls. 55

7. Independent Study and Community Colleges:
   Local Resources for Distance Learners 69

8. Online Study Resources:
   Finding Your Way Through the Jungle 79

PART III: ACCELERATED LEARNING. 89

9. The Power of Accelerated Learning:
   An Introduction 93

10. Reading Power:
    Breaking Through the 400 Barrier 97

11. Memory Power:
    Unlocking Your Brain 107

12. Writing Power:
    Structure, Style, and Speed 121

13. Test-Taking Power:
    Learning to Love the Challenge 131

PART IV: PUTTING IT TOGETHER **141**

14. Choosing Your Path:
    Finding the College That Fits You Best 143

15. Scholarships and Grants:
    Calculating the Costs and Finding the Funds 155

16. Maximum Efficiency:
    Organizing Yourself and Your Surroundings 163

17. Mapping a Course:
    A Strategy for Your College Success 173

PART V: THE MOUNTAINTOP **189**

18. Graduation Point:
    Your Degree and Beyond 191

ABOUT THE AUTHOR **195**

Appendix A:
    Glossary of Distance-Learning Terms 196

Appendix B:
    Credit-by-Examination Programs 202

Appendix C:
    *Degrees and Courses Available Online
    and Through Correspondence Study* 208

Appendix D:
    Degree-Planning Worksheets 214

Appendix E:
    Internet Resources 218

Appendix F:
    Accrediting Agencies 224

INDEX **236**

STUDENT SUCCESS CATALOG **242**

ACKNOWLEDGMENTS

The goal of any education should be to obtain wisdom. Many wise people have influenced me, but the wisdom of the Bible has had the greatest impact on my life. It gave me a love of principles, motivation to do what's right, and a desire to become a godly leader. The lessons of the Bible are timeless, eternal truths that have just as much power and relevance for the twenty-first century as they did for the first century. No education is complete without an understanding of Biblical truth. I will always be indebted to the message of this amazing Book.

A big collective thanks to Karin Brough, David Schwind, Andrew Cope, David Beroth, Heidi Caasi, Ingrid Dahl, Dan Pinkerton, Alexandra Swann, Ronald Illingworth, Robert Herbster, Ronald Schiesz, Howard Berg, and Andrew Pudewa, for all your individual contributions and suggestions in shaping the final manuscript.

I am especially grateful to the following individuals:

Ken Zagone, a man of great vision who was willing to begin dreaming and working with me during the very early stages of this project.

Gentry Stanley, a mentor and friend who encourages me to think outside the box and tackle big projects.

Daniel Bartsch, my faithful line editor who tirelessly reworked and polished my manuscript.

Jim Voeller, for building my faith and for helping me to articulate my ideas for maximum impact.

Bronwyn Pellascio, for giving life to the analogies in this book.

Erik Bonstrom, Jared Yates, and Kyle Yates, three bright students of tremendous vision, for their wit, enthusiasm, and wonderful feedback.

David Voeller, a supportive brother and best friend, especially for producing many of the graphics throughout.

Danielle and Lindsay Voeller, for going above and beyond the call of duty as my sisters to pitch in with every aspect of this project.

I dedicate this book to my parents, Jim and Lori Voeller, who gave me the courage to pursue my life purpose and patiently taught me the character that it takes to become an accelerated distance learner.

Introduction

I've never considered myself as being exceptionally smart, yet I was able to earn my bachelor's degree in six months at a total cost of under $5,000. What's more, I am convinced that I received a better education than most students receive through a traditional four-year college program. How? I applied the revolutionary principles of Accelerated Distance Learning. My total learning experience was so unique that I wrote this book in order to explain the principles of Accelerated Distance Learning to others. You see, generally, when someone hears about my accomplishment, they assume that I have some unique gift or ability. I am here to tell you that if *you* follow the principles in this book, you can do exactly what I did—earn an accredited four-year degree in six months—or even less!

WHAT'S IN THIS BOOK?

In this book, I've attempted to give you all the information you will need to duplicate this accomplishment: I will explain that there is no reason why you can't earn your bachelor's degree in less than six months and for less than $5,000. You will learn exactly how to choose and enroll in a distance-learning program. But, more importantly, you will receive detailed explanations of all of the accelerated learning techniques that will allow you to move through your degree program in record time. Throughout this book, I will also be challenging you to develop a bigger vision for your future, to go further in your education, to experience more of life, to develop an entrepreneurial attitude, and to aspire to leadership.

In order to effectively communicate the methods that I used, I have chosen to create an analogy throughout the book, comparing this new approach to education to the experiences of a hiker. I think you will find many of your own experiences in Accelerated Distance Learning to be similar to the adventures of this hiking pioneer as he braves new territory, discovers faster ways to move along the trail, and realizes the accomplishment of his goal.

As you read this book, think of me as your guide. I have already traveled the trails of Accelerated Distance Learning. My own story is woven into these pages with many practical tips that I've found to be successful. I've learned which trails are good and which should be avoided. I have also included the helpful advice of other accelerated distance learners and educational experts.

AN OUTLINE OF THE BOOK:

PART I lays the framework for the rest of the book, explaining the paradigm shift occurring today in education and the principles that are behind Accelerated Distance Learning.

PART II covers some of the most valuable information you will need as you pursue your education: distance-learning methods. These will allow you to get credit for knowledge you've already obtained and to efficiently learn new information without being stuck in a classroom.

PART III teaches you how to accelerate your learning to speeds faster than you could ever imagine.

PART IV explains how to get organized and put everything you've learned in this book into a detailed, degree-completion plan.

Finally, PART V examines how your journey through Accelerated Distance Learning has prepared you for the challenges and opportunities that await you.

Throughout this book, I will attempt to point you to other resources and tools you will need. The *Student Success Catalog,* located in the Appendix, contains descriptions of the most helpful resources available to students desiring to pursue their education through Accelerated Distance Learning.

HOW IS THIS BOOK DIFFERENT?

Until now, books on distance learning have had two major limitations:

1. THEY HAVE BEEN ADDRESSED PRIMARILY TO STUDENTS WHO ARE PURSUING GRADUATE DEGREES. This book is focused on how to earn a bachelor's degree. The principles of this book will also help you obtain an advanced degree, although it is chiefly concerned with undergraduate studies.

2. THEY ONLY TELL HALF THE STORY. Many books attempt to explain distance learning, however, they don't complete the story by outlining how to use distance learning effectively—by combining it with accelerated learning techniques. Distance education united with accelerated learning techniques will open doors into an entirely new educational universe!

WHO SHOULD READ THIS BOOK?

If you are currently in high school and plan to enroll in college, this book will help you make sense of all the educational decisions you are facing and assist you in jump-starting your college education.

If you are a high school graduate who plans to enroll in college, this book will help you map out an efficient course of study that will save you years of time and thousands of dollars.

If you are already enrolled in college, working toward a bachelor's degree, this book is for you. By applying the principles you find here, you will be able to accelerate your studies and speed ahead of your classmates.

If you are a concerned parent who wants to help your son or daughter avoid the shortcomings and pitfalls of a traditional campus-based college experience, this book provides a proven track to use as an alternative. You will help your student to earn a degree quickly, while saving them from a lifetime of student loans.

FINAL WORD

The information you are about to receive is probably quite different than the preconceived notions you have about college and how students get an education. Be prepared to have these notions challenged, accept change, and try new things.

Accelerated Distance Learning is a proven method for quickly earning your college degree. However, very few people are aware that it exists, and even fewer have put this method into practice. Certainly, there is tremendous opportunity for becoming a pioneer in this new paradigm of education. Pioneers must be willing to step out in a new direction and lead the way. Now this is *your opportunity* to become a pioneer and begin leading the way.

If you are willing to do this, the message of this book will be a tremendous benefit to your life. I encourage you now to read it, apply it, and experience the benefits of Accelerated Distance Learning in your education and in your life.

Your fellow accelerated distance learner and personal trail guide,

Brad Voeller

San Antonio, Texas
May, 2006

BLAZING A NEW TRAIL

You've been planning for the start of this trip for many years. But now, right in front of you, the trailhead marker gives startling information. The words "Graduation Point" are carved and painted on the sign, but there is something here that is unexpected.

What has captured your attention is the number of miles the sign indicates (239) and the fact that it is pointing to a trail that takes off to the south. Something must be wrong. You have studied a map, and you know that Graduation Point is only 53 miles away and lies to the west. Clearly there has been a mistake.

You look around, surprised that you seem to be the only one of many hikers near the trailhead to find the sign odd. Seeing your bewildered look, another hiker walks over.

"What's the problem?" he asks with a chuckle. "Haven't you seen a trailhead marker before? Oh, by the way, my name is Nick."

"Oh, hi," you reply, introducing yourself. "Uh, Nick, this is a mistake, right? I mean, surely these hikers aren't following this *marker to Graduation Point?"*

Nick looks in the direction of the trailhead where several groups of hikers, weighted down with brightly colored backpacks, were disappearing around a bend in the trail.

"Well, yes," he replies, "that is the general idea. In fact, that's where I'm headed right now. If you're worried about making the long journey alone, don't worry. You can travel with my group."

"Well, thanks for the offer, but I'm not planning to take this trail at all. You see, hiking has been an interest of mine for quite some time, and hiking to Graduation Point and beyond has been a dream of mine for years. I've found a Guide Book that gives me the most up-to-date methods in fast travel, and I've studied topographical maps to know the most direct route. I plan to get to Graduation Point—but not by Trail Normal."

As you speak, you can see that Nick isn't convinced. His friendly smile turns into a smirk.

"Well, I hate to throw cold water on your enthusiasm, but I doubt you'll make it. These trails have been here for years, and many hikers have made it to the top. I happen to know there are several sheer cliffs which these trails circumvent. Also, there are no side tours, campsites, or cleared paths. If you travel as the crow flies, you'll be on your own." Nick chuckles and adds, "Half the fun is who you walk with!"

"This isn't about fun," you say to yourself.

By this time, Nick is at the trailhead. Turning around he shouts, "Hope you change your mind and catch up with the rest of us!" as he hurries out of sight.

"Change my mind? Choose to take longer paths, pay tour guides for directions I can get myself, and travel with slow hikers? I'd be crazy to take Trail Normal!"

With new resolve you set out on your journey, heading directly west. The fresh air in your lungs has filled you with a sense of adventure as you begin hiking. Every step brings you closer to Graduation Point.

If you are making plans for college, you have arrived at a critical juncture in your trail. The decisions you make now will dramatically influence the rest of your life. If you really want the best and are not content to simply follow the crowd and do what's expected, this is the Guide Book for you. Most students never even stop to consider that there is a shorter trail leading to their destination, but in this book you will find proven methods for earning the credentials you need in a fraction of the time. By choosing this route you will be pioneering a new way and setting the course for other twenty-first century students to follow.

In this section we'll examine the current changes within our world and how they affect your educational choices, the principles that should guide your educational pursuits, and the traps that will keep you from reaching your destination. I'll also share my own story with you of how I came to learn and apply the methods of Accelerated Distance Learning.

I'm excited for you! You are about to embark on a journey of discovery that will truly result in the realization of your dreams.

The Paradigm Shift:

*Why Accelerated Distance Learning Is THE
Educational Strategy for the Information Age*

O ur world is changing at an unprecedented pace. We have left the industrial age that brought electricity and automobiles and have entered the information age of microcomputers and satellites. While the changes resultin g from the industrial era were great, the advances currently resulting from our society's entrance into the information age are far more spectacular.

Have you ever considered the incredible magnitude of the changes that are taking place in the world of business? Even small companies have become "international" as they purchase and sell products around the world; more and more, employees are able to "telecommute" to work through the Internet; and E-commerce already generates over $132 billion in revenues worldwide and is expanding rapidly.

But what about the field of education? Has the availability and methodology of education also been affected by the arrival of the information age? Definitely! At its core, education parallels the foundational principles of information technology: the transmission of information and ideas. Considering that one of the goals of education is to effectively communicate new truth, it is ironic that there is such a strong tendency to cling to the old system.

In order to understand these technological changes, let's consider the basic facts about information technology and the implications for the world of higher education.

1. **Information technology requires minimal capital investment.** While most industries rely on expensive buildings, factories, and equipment, information technology does not require great resources.

Considering that one of the goals of education is to effectively communicate new truth, it is ironic that there is such a strong tendency to cling to the old system.

*"The world hates change, yet it is the only thing that has brought progress."
—Charles Kettering*

2. **Information technology operates with greater efficiency.** Traditional colleges that must maintain large physical structures are unable to compete with the new distance-learning programs.

3. **Information technology favors smaller, specialized enterprises.** In the past, large, internationally-recognized schools were able to attract students because they provided "one-stop shopping." Myriads of courses and intellectual talent could be found in one place. Today, students can shop at schools from around the globe for high-quality online courses that fit in with their degree program. Small schools, or even a single professor, specializing in offering a certain course, can potentially reach a huge audience. Once the course is completed, the student simply transfers the credit to the school from which he plans to graduate. With this resulting new competition for students, the scales are tipped in favor of smaller colleges and programs that are flexible and highly-specialized.

4. **Information technology makes up-to-date information readily accessible.** With today's technology it is possible to transfer knowledge gleaned through research directly to the people who need it most almost simultaneously with its discovery. For the farmer in South Africa facing crop devastation from a mysterious disease, help that was once a world away is now easily accessible through a search on the Internet. A rural medical practitioner can interact with specialists in nutrition, pathology, and surgical techniques. Students don't need to study outdated textbooks—the latest research is available online!

5. **Information technology promotes remote collaboration.** Unlike the assembly lines of the industrial era that brought huge numbers of workers together in one physical location, work projects in the information age are dispersed through networks that can bring thousands and even millions of people together quickly. While these projects may involve only a few hours of work or several weeks—the amazing thing is that people no longer have to be in one location to work together effectively and efficiently. The implication of all this for education is that classrooms located in expensive campus settings are becoming obsolete. Learners can congregate online.

Do these developments seem incredible? These are not predictions of the future—they are actually happening today! It is only a matter of time, very little time, before these trends become widespread and commonplace. The market for online education is projected to reach $11.5 billion by 2003.

THE TEN PRINCIPLES OF LEARNING

These changes are happening all around us. The big question is, "What does it mean to me, and how do I prepare?" It is generally true that during a time of radical change, those who are prepared and anticipating the new order are the ones who become the leaders of the next generation. Perhaps the greatest way to prepare for the changes that are underway is to gain a firm handle on the ten underlying principles of learning. These ten principles of learning hold true, no matter what the future will bring. These ten principles will be referred to at various points throughout the book. For now, let's look at an overview of the "Ten Principles of Learning."

1. **RESPONSIBILITY.** *You, and you alone, are responsible for your education.* Most students believe that if they just place themselves in the hands of a good school with qualified teachers and faithfully attend class, after four years they will have a good education. Nothing could be further from the truth. It is not the job of a teacher or school to make you learn. It's up to you; it's your responsibility. That's why I show in this book how to take control over the many educational choices available to you. You'll learn how to make a detailed Accelerated Distance Learning plan that allows you to reach your educational goals.

2. **THOROUGHNESS.** *You must examine the accuracy of everything you learn.* Too many times, students tend to unquestioningly receive and believe whatever they read from the printed page. A true learner will develop the art of considering whether what is being presented is indeed accurate. This quality of discernment is readily developed in accelerated distance learners because they are exposed to a variety of texts and perspectives.

3. **EFFICIENCY.** *Accelerated learning takes energy expended in the learning process and makes you more productive.* Accelerated learning techniques will form a foundation for all of your studies and enable you to learn faster and more effectively than you thought possible. We'll take a detailed look at these methods in Part III.

Perhaps the greatest way to prepare for the changes that are underway is to gain a firm handle on the ten underlying principles of learning.

"Responsibility for learning belongs to the student, regardless of age." —Robert Martin

4. **EXPERIENCE.** *Life experience is the best teacher.* The more you can structure your learning around life experiences, the more successful you'll be in preparing for your future work. Every accelerated distance learner should take advantage of the internships, apprenticeships, and work opportunities available in their area of interest. The timesaving techniques in this book will enable you to spend much less time doing "school" and free you up to concentrate on the learning that takes place through life experiences. This is the beauty of earning credits through portfolio assessment. Many colleges are now willing to grant credit in recognition of the valuable education that is gained through the experiences of life. We'll be looking more closely at portfolio assessment in Chapter 4.

5. **LIFELONG LEARNING.** *The amount of information in man's store of knowledge is exploding at an increasing rate of growth—you must keep up.* Because of this proliferation of knowledge, even keeping up with one's own area of expertise is becoming increasingly difficult. Add to this the desire that we all have to learn more in other areas, and we are quickly faced with an impossible situation. Our only hope is to develop the essential skills required to become an efficient and successful, lifelong learner. Few people develop this skill. As you succeed in this and view all of life as a learning experience, you will stand apart from the crowd.

6. **GLOBAL PERSPECTIVE.** *The revolution that has taken place in the world's information and communication systems requires that we develop a global perspective on life.* The information revolution is shrinking the world. Increasingly, people of other languages and cultures cross our path, and we must develop the skills that are necessary to understand and appreciate them. Accelerated Distance Learning will connect you with fascinating students, teachers, and experts from around the globe in what has become a virtual classroom. In addition to online cross-cultural interaction, the time and money that is saved through Accelerated Distance Learning will enable you to travel the world and broaden your understanding of other cultures.

7. **UNDERSTANDING.** *The goal of education is to reach a higher level of understanding.* True education is not proven by being able to recite a set of facts and figures; it is demonstrated when

one understands how those facts relate to each other. There is no virtue, and certainly no education, in simply listening to a lecture or reading a book, and then regurgitating it all for an exam. A true learner will not just memorize facts. They will mull them over, analyze them, and look at them from different perspectives. You must develop the foundational skill of asking questions about whatever it is that you're studying. This will result in better retention and comprehension of the information. Developing this skill will result in quality understanding which is vital for any leader.

8. **CUSTOMIZED LEARNING.** *Education should be customized to your learning style and needs.* Faced with the limitations of budgets, facilities, and staff, traditional institutions of higher learning have not been able to provide "custom made" education for individual learners. Technology now allows accelerated distance learners to select the teachers who will provide the best instruction and guidance for their individual goals, interests, and learning style. Students are no longer limited to the teachers in the college from which their degree will be granted!

9. **INFLUENCE.** *One life can make an impact in the world.* Information technology places the potential for worldwide influence in the hands of individuals. As an accelerated distance learner, it is likely that your potential for influence will be even greater. Your education will uniquely prepare you to think independently and serve as a leader in society.

10. **MOTIVATION.** *The true success of any achievement will be proven by the presence or absence of proper motivation.* As an accelerated distance learner you will master accelerated learning techniques, use distance-learning methods, and ultimately get your degree. These are noble goals to pursue, however, you will never experience the full potential of these achievements without the proper motivation for your pursuit. We'll examine this important topic of life purpose and motivation in Chapter 2.

These ten vital principles should guide every academic choice. Throughout life we will each face decisions to either follow principles and achieve success, or ignore them and experience regret.

There is a story that wonderfully illustrates the importance of basing decisions on principles. One cold, winter night the captain of an oceango-

Principles are like lighthouses. They are always there to give us direction, and they never move or change.

ing vessel saw what he thought were the lights of another ship directly in his path. The captain radioed to the ship, "This is the captain speaking. You are in great danger. Change your course immediately."

The reply came back, "This is the lighthouse speaking. Change course yourself—you're the one in danger!"

Principles are like lighthouses. They are always there to give us direction and they never move or change. Recognize these ten principles; embrace them, and you will not only survive, but thrive during this day of dramatic change in higher education.

The Traps of Traditional Education:

What They Are and How to Avoid Them

I n the last chapter we learned about the dramatic changes taking place in the world and the vital importance of building our lives on unchanging principles. In this chapter, we'll look at the seven traps, or "syndromes," that students often develop when they ignore the principles. Also, I'll share with you how I avoided the syndromes and became an accelerated distance learner.

Principle #1: RESPONSIBILITY. You, and you alone, are responsible for your education.

SEVEN SYNDROMES: COMMON PATTERNS FOR FAILURE AMONG STUDENTS

I have talked with many discouraged students; sadly, most of them did not pursue their education according to the ten principles that were outlined in the first chapter. Their discouragement stemmed from getting caught in one of the following common syndromes:

1. SOLDIER SYNDROME. When soldiers march in step they have trouble making sudden turns. Many students have the same problem. They are locked into an educational system that doesn't allow them to keep up with changes that occur every day in our society. This syndrome is usually the result of ignorance rather than a conscious choice.

2. TOURIST SYNDROME. Tourists usually travel in groups and rarely venture off to explore on their own. As a student in the twenty-first century, you must be willing to venture off and pursue learning experiences that fit your individual learning style. Stick with the group, and you may miss some of life's greatest learning opportunities.

"The person who really wants to do something finds a way, the other person finds an excuse." —Anonymous

11

3. **DRIFTER SYNDROME.** I'm amazed how many students think that it's the school's job to make them learn. These drifters can't figure out why they don't get better grades and all the knowledge they will need by just showing up in class. When life brings along unexpected situations, they respond by thinking, "I never learned that in school; what do I do now?"

4. **OLD-TIMER SYNDROME.** The common advice of the day is, "Borrow money, go to college for four years, and get a job in corporate America." This viewpoint is bound by old paradigms and does not recognize the significance of the changes in our society. Just because "we've always done it that way," doesn't mean that the old course is the best course.

5. **WANDERER SYNDROME.** The wanderer believes that genius is predetermined at birth. They wander aimlessly through life with no goals and no aspirations, thinking that they lack intelligence. But genius is not about IQ, natural ability, or genetic make-up. As Thomas Edison said, "Genius is 2% inspiration and 98% perspiration." With diligence, accelerated learning techniques, and a bigger vision for the future, anyone can become an excellent student.

6. **HOME BODY SYNDROME.** Some students aren't very adventurous. Although we live in an age of global opportunity, many are content to go no further than the local junior college for their education. By not pursuing international experiences, they may fail to reach their full potential. Be willing to try methods that are new, uncommon, and even out of your comfort zone.

7. **TAKER SYNDROME.** Of the many people I have met that are frustrated, discouraged, and discontent, one common factor has stood out: their wrong motivations. When life becomes solely motivated by the pursuit of possessions and personal pleasures, an emptiness will soon follow. I encourage every accelerated distance learner to aim for something much higher—become a giver not a taker.

While the names that I have attached to these syndromes may be unfamiliar to you, they are all very real, and most students succumb to one or more of them. Our society has (perhaps unintentionally) programmed us to accept the status quo. Every day we are bombarded by messages that subliminally say, "Go with the crowd." "Don't try to do new and innovative things."

"Learning is boring and hard." "Looking out for number one is the only way to survive." "Your life is the product of a series of accidents."

Because this book challenges each of these statements, it may initially appear to present a radical approach to education. My message is admittedly different. However, those who are willing to listen and try a new way will experience rich rewards.

HOW I AVOIDED THE SYNDROMES

These learning syndromes are easy to fall into, however, they can be avoided. The only reason that I didn't succumb to them was because I listened to the wise advice of my parents and mentors, who challenged me to think about learning "outside the box." I will always be indebted to them.

During my teenage years my parents and I began to seriously evaluate my future and the educational choices that lay before me. My parents continually encouraged me to consider each day of life as a learning experience. Through their influence, I was able to identify and avoid the trap of thinking that true learning takes place only in the classroom. I spent several years completing internships that taught me a broad range of very practical knowledge and skills. I acquired landscaping skills by developing a landscaping company. I learned home building by working for a construction company, law and government by serving as an intern with my state representative, and sales and marketing by working for my dad. Not only did these experiences provide an excellent foundation for future learning, but I had fun in the process!

When I turned eighteen, I almost embraced the false idea that all learners are cut out of the same mold and that I should group myself with others in a college setting. Most of my friends were enrolling in traditional college programs, and I was feeling pressure to do the same. Thankfully, my parents saw that I first needed to better understand my purpose in life before continuing to pursue formal academics. They encouraged me to continue broadening my foundation by seeking a variety of real-life learning experiences.

An opportunity opened up for me to spend several months working in the Philippines. Interwoven through all my activities and service projects were opportunities to learn about another nation's language, culture, history, societal pressures, and trends. I began to consider my own culture and society from a new point of view. No longer did I have a limited frame of reference for life; international experience had taught me to think and act from a global perspective.

"Destiny is not a matter of chance, it is a matter of choice." —William Jennings Bryan

I spent several years completing internships that taught me a broad range of very practical knowledge and skills.

"A man must consider what a rich realm he abdicates when he becomes a conformist." —Ralph Waldo Emerson

Within a short time, my ability to memorize and recall information quadrupled, my concentration powers were sharpened, and my reading speed went through the roof!

My learning experiences up to this point had increased my desire to learn. However, I did have a nagging sense that maybe I didn't have what it takes—I felt I wasn't smart enough to learn the skills I needed, certainly not as quickly as I believed necessary. When a friend introduced me to a memory and speed reading program, I immediately knew that I had the answer. (We will learn more about this in SECTION III: Accelerated Learning.) Within a short time, my ability to memorize and recall information quadrupled, my concentration powers were sharpened, and my reading speed went through the roof! Suddenly, a new world of learning that previously seemed impossible opened before me.

Later, I accepted an opportunity to go to China for six months and work as an English teacher. Realizing how beneficial my prior experience in the Philippines had been, I was eager for this new adventure. During my stay in China I taught, traveled, and studied, trying to absorb the many sights and sounds. My life was deeply impacted as I observed China's struggle to develop and sensed that the people there are searching for direction. As I worked with young Chinese businesspeople, a desire began growing in my heart to teach them sound business principles and skills, while at the same time encouraging them to use their businesses to benefit their countrymen.

I knew that I had learned a tremendous amount through all my life experiences, but would anyone recognize this learning?

When I returned from China I felt that I had the purpose and direction I needed, but it still seemed like a brick wall was blocking my path. I knew that I had learned a tremendous amount through all my life experiences, but would anyone recognize this learning? I wanted to pursue my calling through teaching and consulting, but how could I do this without a recognized credential? I started searching for a way to accomplish my goals without having to jump through all the traditional college hoops.

It was at this point that I discovered distance learning. When I realized that it is possible to earn an accredited degree quickly, inexpensively, and conveniently, I could hardly contain my enthusiasm! I enrolled in Thomas Edison College, one of the top schools specializing in distance education, and began working toward the completion of my B.S. in Business Administration with a specialization in International Management. In less than a month, I earned my first thirty credits by taking exams that tested the knowledge which I had already acquired. I began to prepare summaries of some of the experiences that I had and made comparisons to the content of various college courses. By doing this, I received college credit for my prior learning experience through a method called "portfolio assessment." For more specialized courses like International Economics, I completed correspondence courses and did independent studies with local professors.

About this time, I discovered that distance-learning methods are completely compatible with accelerated learning techniques. In fact, they are made for each other! This new concept, Accelerated Distance Learning, allowed me to earn my bachelor's degree in less than six months at a cost of less than $5,000!

Accelerated Distance Learning has not only allowed me to earn my degree quickly, it is now helping me to fulfill my life purpose. I have had the privilege of founding Global Leadership Institute, Inc. This nonprofit organization and its subsidiary, Global Learning Strategies, are devoted to internationally equipping wise and skillful leaders through Accelerated Distance Learning.

This is radical thinking! The idea of completing an accredited college degree in six months, at a cost of less than $5,000, while developing a photographic memory, and reading at speeds of several thousand words per minute may seem impossible to you. As incredible as it sounds, none of it is beyond your grasp. If you determine to apply yourself to obtaining and using the skills that are explained in this book, nothing will stop you from reaching your educational goals.

My desire is that you will succeed. Even beyond that, I hope that you will be ready to share your success with others and use your accomplishments to free those who are trapped in the old patterns of life. You are only limited by your own small ambitions.

"The impossible is so often the untried."
—Jim Goodwin

"Impossibility is a word only to be found in the dictionary of fools."
—Napoleon Bonaparte

DISTANCE LEARNING

Left, right, left, right. Your stride settles into a steady pace, eating up the miles. Of course, pace really depends on terrain.

And did you ever see a variety of terrains! First, as you are leaving Trail Normal behind, the ground slopes gently into rolling hills. The hiking there is fairly easy until, suddenly, the hills end, and you come to a shallow river.

You decide to cross the North Fork, avoiding the desert terrain toward the South. Wading the river is difficult, and the sharp edges of rocky shale on the other side require slow, cautious steps. However, the rock soon changes to sand, and sand to forest floor, and your pace picks up again. In no time, you are hiking faster than on the slopes!

"This is great!" you say to yourself, as your hiking boots crunch the pine needle carpet. The forest is a pleasant place to hike, you won't have to endure the burning sun, and the unusual species of trees fascinate you. Soon, the creek you are following empties into a pond.

"Perfect fishing hole," you muse, as your stomach reminds you of lunchtime. "I'll just throw in a few casts to see if I can get a bite."

With skillful fingers, you tie a fly on your line and let out a perfect cast onto the glasslike surface of the pond. That was Uncle Phil's signature cast; the one you'd perfected during fishing trips with him as a kid. After another cast, a large trout is tugging on your line. Those experiences from earlier in life are sure coming in handy now.

Just as there are a variety of terrains in hiking toward a final destination, so there are a variety of ways that you will be able to accumulate credits as you travel toward your degree goal through distance education.

Distance learning—exactly what is it? Simply put, distance learning is the method of obtaining your training through schools and instructors that are remote from you. The number of choices that are available to you through distance learning are numerous and can be quite confusing. As with any journey, there are different sets of directions which may be followed, each one presenting its own unique set of challenges, experiences, and time commitments.

The encouraging thing is that there are directions that can help you work quickly and economically toward your goal. Yes, you can get a fully accredited degree through distance learning that is just as respected as those earned through more traditional means. With over 450,000 courses currently offered and many different ways of earning credits, your choices are practically endless.

In this section we'll examine each method of accumulating credits in detail, talk about their respective benefits, and offer many practical tips to ensure that your journey is a success.

Credit-by-Examination:

The Best-Kept Secret in Higher Education

U sually, there are three phases to a college course. There is the classroom instruction, the testing that follows, and ultimately, the credit that is granted upon successful completion. Through credit-by-examination, you will be able to skip the instructional phase of this sequence. Many times, required courses for college are simply a review of advanced high school courses, or they provide instruction in an area that has already been mastered. Instead of sitting through sixteen weeks of lectures on material that you already know, credit-by-examination allows you to simply take the test and receive credit! Many tests can be completed in an hour! You won't be able to get all of the credits that you need through testing, but use it whenever you can.

What do you do if you don't know much about the subject? Using the accelerated learning techniques discussed in this book, you will be able to teach yourself much faster than you would have learned in a class. After doing self study, you can take the test and receive the same amount of credit as if you had attended a regular class. Many testing programs help you prepare by providing sample test questions and a list of recommended study resources.

PREPARING FOR THE TESTS

Before deciding to take a particular exam, you will want to verify that your college grants credit for that particular exam. If so, find out the minimum score necessary for credit as well as where and when you can take the test. Most colleges have a department for administering exams; they should be able to answer these questions for you. While some colleges

Credit-by-examination allows you to simply take the test and receive credit!

offer examinations only during certain times of the year, usually you can call up and schedule an exam whenever it's convenient for you. Most community colleges furnish testing rooms and proctors for almost any exam you decide to take.

Continue reading this section of the book and learn about the various ways of earning college credit through distance-learning programs. If, after doing so, you decide to complete a major portion of your degree through credit-by-examination, I recommend that you investigate the following schools: Thomas Edison College, Excelsior College, Ohio University, New York University, and Charter Oak State College. Each school offers its own credit-by-examination program and accepts most other credit-by-examination programs. I encourage you to communicate with our office to receive updated information on which schools accept credit by examination.

Don't wait until you actually enroll in a college to begin taking tests. You can begin earning credit-by-examination before enrolling in a college. Some programs like CLEP allow you to "bank" your credits. Once you select a college, you will be able to fill out a simple form requesting that the transcript of your credits be sent to your college for evaluation.

Don't wait until you actually enroll in a college to begin taking tests.

In order to receive a passing score, adequate test preparation is critical. The amount of time it takes to prepare will depend on how much of the course content you already know and how skilled you have become in using the accelerated learning techniques described in Part III.

I always started my test preparation by reviewing study guides, sample tests, and other preparation materials. If there were sample tests available, I took them early in my preparations to determine areas where I was weak. Then, I would focus my studies on the areas of weakness.

As I began my studies I always obtained an examination guide for the course. Most examination guides list recommended texts for study. Because most tests are general in scope, not testing on the specific information from one particular textbook, you will be wise to use two or more textbooks, per subject, when preparing for your tests.

CREDIT-BY-EXAMINATION PROGRAM OVERVIEWS

Here are descriptions of some of the best credit-by-examination programs. A listing of all examination titles offered through each program is in Appendix B.

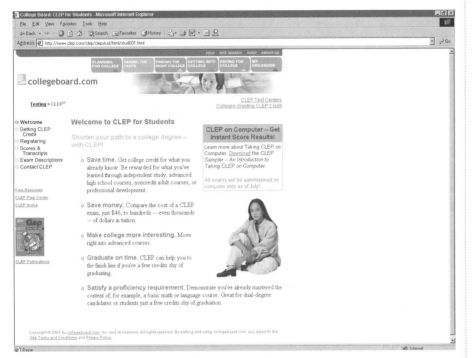

Start earning college credits through CLEP.

CLEP

The College-Level Examination Program, or CLEP, is probably the most widely known of all of the available testing programs. CLEP tests have been used by more students (over four million) and are accepted by more schools (over 2,900) than any other program.

There are five general CLEP exams and thirty subject exams. Each of the tests are in a 90-minute, multiple-choice format, except for the essay portion of the English Composition test.

The five general exams are equivalent to the first, full year of college. Regardless of the major which you choose, these exams will almost always fulfill the requirements of the degree program that you will complete. If the school you have selected accepts them, I strongly recommend that you take all five general CLEP exams.

The subject exams cover material from the fields of business, composition and literature, foreign languages, history and social science, and science and mathematics. The questions are more in-depth than those in the general exams, so you will need a more complete knowledge of the subject in order to obtain a passing score.

A friend of mine, working part time, was able to complete the five general CLEP exams, a year's worth of college credit, in less than two months.

After you decide where to take your CLEP test, contact the proctor, provide your name and phone number, and ask the proctor to order the test you need. On the test date, take your photo ID (driver's license, passport, or college ID), along with a $60 check made out to CLEP, and some cash (usually $10–$20) for the test center's registration fee. If you plan to take CLEP tests, you can leave your pencils at home. The tests are now offered via computer, and you're able to get a grade (unofficial) immediately after taking the test!

The school where you have enrolled will determine the number of credits you will receive for each exam. Generally, if you attempt to answer all of the questions and get at least 60% correct, you will have achieved a passing score and will receive full credit for the exam. Most colleges award six credits for each of the general exams and three for each subject exam.

Here are some important tips on how to attain higher CLEP scores:

- In CLEP's multiple-choice format, there is no penalty for wrong answers. Even if you don't know the answer and are unable to eliminate one of the choices, make a guess. Don't leave any questions unanswered.

- Try to eliminate even one wrong answer, make your best guess between all the others. Don't leave the question unanswered.

- Don't look for trick questions: all of the questions are straightforward and mean just what they say.

- Keep moving. Each question carries equal weight, so don't spend too long on an especially difficult one.

- Read all four choices before you answer. More than one answer might be correct. The CLEP instructions ask you to pick the *best* choice.

SPECIAL TECHNIQUE: If you aren't currently enrolled in a college, start taking CLEP tests anyway. CLEP will accumulate your test scores for you. After selecting your college, call the college's admissions or testing office to find out which courses you can bypass through CLEP exams, what scores are required for credit, and the number of credit hours that will be granted. When you send CLEP $15, they will forward a transcript of all your CLEP test scores to the college. If you are able to pass many tests, the time of your enrollment and your tuition bill will be significantly reduced.

Contact CLEP directly to locate the nearest CLEP testing location and to obtain a free copy of their publication, *Information for Candidates.*

Most colleges award six credits for each of the general exams and three for each subject exam.

TIP: Don't study too narrowly for the CLEP general exams. Try to acquire a broad knowledge of the subject.

P.O. Box 6600
Princeton, NJ 08541-6000
clep@ets.org
Fax (609) 771-7088
Phone (609) 771-7865

See the *Student Success Catalog* at the end of this book to find out how you can obtain a copy of *The Official CLEP Study Guide for the CLEP Examinations.*

Excelsior College Examinations

Excelsior College offers more than forty examinations on a variety of subjects worth 3 to 8 credits each. Although more expensive than CLEP ($100 to $360 per test) they still cost just a fraction of what most students pay per credit for classroom-based courses.

If your major is nursing or healthcare-related, you'll be especially interested in this program. Currently, Excelsior has eighteen exams for healthcare-related subjects!

There are over 400 Prometric Testing Centers that serve as test sites for Excelsior Exams. Prometric makes the testing process simple. The computerized multiple-choice exam is scored immediately. Unlike other tests, you will not have to wait six weeks for the results.

Excelsior Exams are widely accepted by colleges and universities around the world. Before you register for an exam, I recommend that you contact your school and make sure that they accept the exam and that it qualifies as a valid replacement for a required course.

Call the number below to register for an exam or request an information packet. After registration you'll be sent a letter authorizing you to take tests for the next twelve months at the Prometric Testing Center of your choice. Once registered, you'll be able to call the testing center and schedule your exam at your convenience.

For more information about Excelsior Exams:
1-888-723-9267
www.excelsior.edu

Or for more information about Prometric Testing Centers:
1-800-479-5606
www.2test.com

TIP: If you take the English Composition exam, take the version with the essay. Some colleges accept only the test with the essay, and most students score better on the essay version. Be sure to plan ahead for this test though; unlike all other CLEP tests, the English Composition with Essay exam is only offered in January, April, June, and October. Since essays are hand-graded, it takes longer to receive the test results than the usual three to six weeks for other CLEP exams.

Excelsior Exams are widely accepted by colleges and universities around the world.

Excelsior College examinations are another great way to begin earning college credits.

DANTES Subject Standardized Tests (DSSTs)

Originally developed for U.S. military personnel, these 30 multiple-choice examinations are now available to civilians. DSSTs are administered at over 600 locations worldwide and are accepted by over 1,200 colleges and universities. I found that the easiest place to take DSSTs was at a military base. The base where I went scheduled three testing periods every week. All I had to do was show up on time (the military is strict, so don't show up a minute late!) with a photo I.D. and a check made out to DANTES, and I could take the test of my choice. Potentially, you could take up to three DSSTs a week if you wanted.

Once I made the mistake of showing up two minutes late for my DANTES exam and was denied entry.

At $60 per three-credit-hour test, DSSTs are an inexpensive method for earning credit. If you don't like the pressure of timed tests, you'll love DSSTs—they have no time limit!

Just like CLEP exams, you don't have to be enrolled in a college to take DSSTs. You can begin taking them at any time.

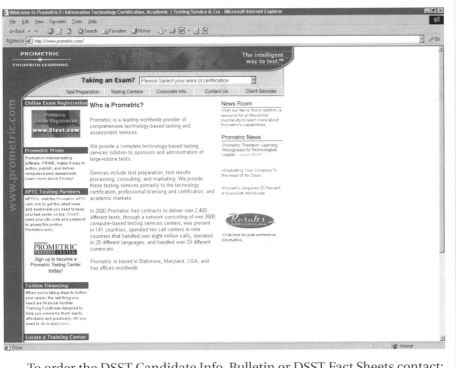

Looking for a place to take your exam? Check out www.prometric.com.

To order the DSST Candidate Info. Bulletin or DSST Fact Sheets contact:

Thomson Prometricl
2000 Lenox Dr., 3rd Floor
Lawrenceville, NJ 08648
Fax (609) 895-5026
Phone (877) 471-9860
www.getcollegecredit.com
www.getcollegecredit.com/04learners_a.htm#FACTSHEETS

At $60 per test, CLEPs and DSSTs are the least expensive methods for earning credit that I have discovered.

Thomas Edison College Examination Program (TECEP)

I have taken more TECEP exams than any other kind. It feels great to take a couple of exams, completing the equivalent of six credit hours of course work in a single afternoon!

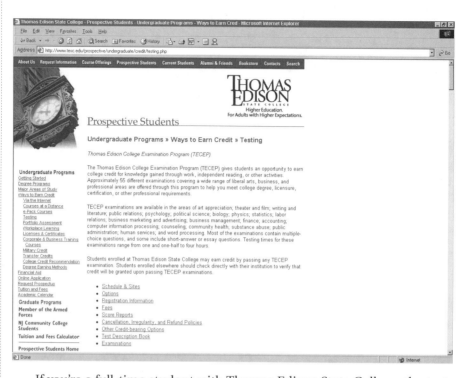

If you're a full-time student with Thomas Edison State College, the tests are covered by the cost of your tuition—otherwise, each three-credit-hour test costs $420 ($140 per credit).

You can arrange to take TECEP exams at a DANTES approved test site or at a nearby college or university. TECEP is one of the most flexible and convenient testing programs, since you choose the date, time, and place for the test.

Unlike most other testing programs, TECEP also offers tests for upper-level courses. Be forewarned though, these tests are more difficult and usually require the completion of prerequisite courses.

If you're planning to take any TECEP exams, I suggest that you get the *Test Description* guides through the following link: http://www.tesc.edu. This handy reference contains everything you need to know about TECEP exams, even a list of recommended textbooks and study aids appropriate for each test. To order your copy or get more information about TECEP contact:

TECEP Registration
Office of Test Administration
Thomas Edison State College

101 W. State St.
Trenton, NJ 08608-1176
(609) 633-2844

Ohio University

Ohio University offers over sixty correspondence courses that can be taken on a credit-by-examination basis. OU allows you to sign up for a course and arrange to have the exam administered by a proctor in your area anytime in the following six months. That's all there is to it! The test will be graded and Ohio University will award college credit.

This program is especially helpful if you're trying to complete an obscure course such as Asian Development Studies or Aviation Science.

When you register, you'll receive a course syllabus, a list of textbooks, and some information about the test. This information will help you save hours of preparation time. It is quite simple to measure your test preparation progress since each test is based on a specific textbook.

The cost of this program is reasonable too: $66 per **quarter** hour credit. (To translate quarter hour credits into semester hours, see the glossary under "Quarter and Semester hours.")

For more information contact:

Office of Independent Study
Tupper Hall
302 Ohio University
Athens, OH 45701
(800) 444-2910
(740) 593-2910 (Voice)
(740) 593-2901 (FAX)
www.ohiou.edu/lifelong
www.ohiou.edu/independent/spec_cce.htm (exam pricing updates)
E-mail: independent.study@ohiou.edu

The New York University Foreign Language Testing Program

Need a fast way to fill a foreign language requirement for your degree program? The New York University Foreign Language Testing Program may

Ohio University offers greater assistance in helping students prepare for exams.

This program is especially helpful if you're trying to complete an obscure course such as Asian Development Studies or Aviation Science.

be for you. This testing program evaluates listening, reading, and writing skills in over fifty languages.

For five months I did volunteer work in the Philippines, and my language skills reached a basic conversation level. I decided to take the test for Tagalog. While I didn't do very well on the listening comprehension or translation, my essay was good enough for a score of ten points. As a result, my school granted me ten credit hours! Not bad for a two-hour exam!

There are two test formats: 12-point and 16-point. You can earn any number of points, from zero up to the full number allowed by the test. Most colleges award one credit for each point.

STUDENT'S POINT OF VIEW: *Credit-by-Examination for Speed*
NAME: *David Schwind*
HOME STATE: *California*
MAJOR: *Bachelor of Science, Business and History*
COLLEGE: *Regents (Excelsior) College*
AGE AT GRADUATION: *22*

Since the time I was a young child, my desire was to serve in the military. Earning college credit through credit-by-examination made this dream a reality.

After enrolling in Regents College's Bachelor of Science program, I established a routine of reading a textbook and taking the related CLEP or DANTES exam on a weekly basis. I was able to take these exams for a small fee at a local university, often completing several at one time. In this manner, I was able to complete over ninety lower-level college credits. For upper-level credits, I took Regents College Exams (RCE). Combined with my lower-level credits, I finally completed my Bachelor's degree with 128 credits.

Instead of spending four years trapped on a college campus, I was able to graduate cum laude with my Bachelor of Science in Business and History, one year and seven months from my date of enrollment!

Was it worth the effort? Undoubtedly! My leadership capacity and responsibilities have greatly expanded since earning my degree and joining the U.S. Navy as an officer. Because I am one of my ship's Division Officers, I am expected to be an outstanding example to my men, and I often have opportunities to provide counsel and encouragement.

I would urge anyone who plans on going into the military to pursue their education through distance learning and begin earning credit through the credit-by-examination method.

On the 12-point exam, students answer questions about a listening comprehension passage, translate it into English and into the test language, and then write a short essay on one of several general topics from several choices that are offered. The 16-point exam has the same format, except you are allowed three hours to take the exam instead of two, and must write a longer, more complex 350-word essay.

The 12-point exam costs $265, while the cost of the 16-point exam is $360. Exams taken off-campus require an additional $20 fee. All you need to do to take the test off-site is have your proctor send NYU a letter agreeing to administer the exam.

To get more information or register for an exam, contact NYU at:

New York University
School of Continuing and Professional Studies
Testing Center
50 Cooper Square, Ste 300
New York, NY 10003
(212) 992-9060
www.scps.nyu.edu

AP Exams

Although Advanced Placement tests were originally developed for high school seniors, they are now available to anyone pursuing college credit. There are now over 35 exams offered across 20 subject areas. The College Board states that, "In 2005, more than 1.2 million students worldwide took more than 2.1 million AP Exams."

This makes AP one of the most popular examination programs. Each exam costs $82 and is worth from 3 to 8 credits each, depending on the standards and policies of your college. You can take AP exams by arranging a testing time with a local high school that offers the exams. Check out their Web site or call their order line to get AP test preparation materials and learn more.

AP
P.O. Box 6671
Princeton, NJ 08541-6671
1-888-225-5427
(609) 771-7300
Order line (609) 771-7243
www.collegeboard.org/ap

Get a jump start on college with AP Exams.

Although Advanced Placement tests were originally developed for high school seniors, they are now available to anyone pursuing college credit.

Graduate Record Exams (GRE)

GRE subject exams are normally taken by students who've completed a baccalaureate degree with a major in one of the GRE subject exam areas. College graduates take the test hoping that a high score will help them get into a graduate study program. However, some schools will also award undergraduate college credit for these exams. Beware—these tests are not easy! Study thoroughly before attempting one.

GRE tests are available at Prometric Testing Centers and many other locations. Contact GRE to find the location nearest you. Each subject exam costs $130, but it is possible to receive as many as 30 credits for one test!

Beware—these tests are not easy! Study thoroughly before attempting one.

Some students have completed their entire degree by just taking three GRE exams and the five general CLEP exams. Using this method, you could theoretically complete your entire bachelor's degree within a few days! If you're interested in this method, contact Excelsior College. They've prepared a list of textbooks for each test and a practice sheet that includes sample questions as well as a description of the examination's content. You can find these at www.excelsior.edu.

To receive the official GRE study materials and more information contact:

GRE-ETS
P.O. Box 6000
Princeton, NJ 08541-6000
Phone: (609) 771-7670   Fax: (609) 771-7906
www.gre.org

GRE—not just for graduate students.

WHAT ARE YOU WAITING FOR?

Through credit-by-examination there's no waiting to apply, no worrying about being accepted, and no fear of filled classes. You can schedule your test today and start next week. If you're in a hurry to complete your degree program, credit-by-examination is definitely the way to go.

Now, *go take your test!*

Portfolio Assessment:

Credit for Real-Life Learning

Principle #4: EXPERIENCE. Life experience is the best teacher.

Often college graduates enter the workforce in their chosen field, only to discover that they are dissatisfied with the life work for which they so diligently prepared. Why does this happen? The failure lies in the traditional method of preparation for one's future. Usually, students select a major based on what they think they might like to do for a living. What is sorely lacking in this method is the opportunity to undergo practical experience in the chosen area of study in order to confirm one's chosen direction. In addition to the inherent problem of being removed from reality, classroom academic studies often prove completely inadequate as preparation for the demands of the real workplace. Traditional classroom learning leans heavily on theory and is almost void of practical application.

For example, a friend of mine thought he wanted to be a teacher. However, after spending four years getting his bachelor's degree, he realized that he didn't know how to relate to children, and, to make matters worse, he didn't even like working in a school setting! He should have taught in a school as an intern to discover if he was really cut out for the job. If he had liked it, he could have turned his life experience into a portfolio and gotten credit for it. If he didn't like it, he could have quickly changed course and avoided years of wasted effort.

If you wanted to learn a skill like rappelling or wilderness survival or mountain climbing, how would you learn it? You would probably spend most of your time practicing and interacting with experts in those skills. Their tips, encouragement, and mentoring would greatly benefit you. Learning skills for use on the job should be no different. And with portfolio assessment, you can get college credit for this "real-life" learning.

"I never let schooling interfere with my education."
—Mark Twain

A REWARDING EXPERIENCE

As I reviewed my life experiences, I realized there were several things I had done that could be categorized in what might be referred to as "International Business Ethics." I had spent a significant amount of time with business students in China, business managers in Taiwan, government leaders in the Philippines, and business consultants in the U.S. The problem was, my school didn't offer a course in International Business Ethics. However, with distance learning, this did not create an obstacle. I found another school that offered a course in International Business Ethics, prepared a portfolio of my experiences and was able to receive credit from my school based on those experiences and my documentation of what I had learned. I know that these real-life work experiences gave me a much greater grasp of the concepts and theories of international business ethics than I would have received in a classroom setting. What's more, I was able to prepare my portfolio in just one week!

WHY PORTFOLIO ASSESSMENT IS SUCH A POWERFUL TOOL

TRUE UNDERSTANDING. Portfolio assessment encourages you to be an active learner, not a passive listener. We'll look more at this important concept in Chapter 9.

FREEDOM FROM THE CLASSROOM. With portfolio assessment, the world is your classroom!

EDUCATION THAT IS UP-TO-DATE. Your learning isn't limited to a few textbooks written some time in the past; you're able to work with the most up-to-date information available in your field of study.

TRUE SOCIALIZATION. You are not limited to the experience or knowledge of a few professors and students who may all have a similar background.

REAL-LIFE EXPERIENCES. Theory about life is a poor substitute for the real thing.

NETWORKING. Portfolio assessment provides a means of building unique, lasting relationships with mentors and fellow students in a way that does not occur in a traditional classroom setting.

ULTIMATE FLEXIBILITY. Your course of study is customized to match your needs and interests.

TIME SAVINGS. You can actually learn a subject and document your educational experience faster than you could through taking a standard course in that subject.

The principle behind portfolio assessment is that actual knowledge and understanding is much more important than the method that is used to acquire knowledge. Portfolio assessment recognizes that learning can take place anywhere, anytime, and in a variety of ways.

WHAT'S YOUR EXPERIENCE?

You'll be surprised at how many of your experiences may qualify for credit. Here are just a few activities that may be eligible. The possibilities are practically endless!

Traveling to Mexico

Speaking Chinese

Organizing a children's program

Teaching Sunday School classes

Starting a small business

Preparing a marketing plan

Preparing and giving a speech

Playing the violin

Landscaping your yard

Remodeling your home

Living in a foreign country

Researching your family history

Writing a book

Attending a seminar

Reading Shakespeare

Taking photographs

Designing Web pages

Singing in a choir

Creating a watercolor painting

Playing in an orchestra

Visiting National Parks

Writing computer programs

Learning sign language

Making furniture

Building a deck

Creating a video

Volunteering in a campaign

Raising animals

Leading a Bible study

FIVE STEPS TO PRODUCING GREAT PORTFOLIOS

Portfolio assessment is neither difficult nor complicated. Here are the five steps of the portfolio process:

STEP 1: Identify your areas of learning.

STEP 2: Identify a college course that is equivalent to your learning experience.

"Experience is one thing that you can't get for nothing."
—Oscar Wilde

Portfolio assessment recognizes that learning can take place anywhere, anytime, and in a variety of ways.

"Experience is not what happens to you; it is what you do with what happens to you."
—Huxley

STEP **3**: Make sure that the credit for the course you have selected fits into your degree program.

STEP **4**: Describe your learning experience in a narrative.

STEP **5**: Present evidence that documents and verifies your learning.

STEP 1: Identify your areas of learning.

It is amazing how many learning experiences each of us have had in life that can be translated into college-level credit. The first step in creating a portfolio is to review your life and make an inventory of your learning experiences. Create an outline of what you have learned and how it compares to college-level learning. Here are some questions to help you brainstorm:

- Have you acquired specialized skills?
- What facts did you need to know?
- How have you demonstrated the skills you acquired?
- Have you operated machinery?
- Have you learned specialized terminology or technical jargon?
- Have you supervised others?
- Have you engaged in problem solving?
- Have you evaluated data?
- Have you given special presentations?
- Have you received training or attended workshops?
- Has your knowledge helped you learn other subjects?

The first step in creating a portfolio is to review your life and make an inventory of your learning experiences.

Use these questions to evaluate experiences such as employment, political activities, non-credit classes, hobbies, church activities, volunteer work, workshops, cultural or artistic pursuits, independent reading, and study.

Do you need to do a portfolio on something you haven't learned yet? Determine what you need to learn to fulfill the course requirement, plan how you will learn it, and document the learning as it takes place. When completed, prepare a portfolio and submit it for credit.

STEP 2: Identify a college course that is equivalent to your learning experience.

Look for colleges that offer courses and award credit for the life experiences that you have had. By examining the course descriptions in college course catalogs, you will be able to find this information. In addition, review the course syllabus, if available—it shows the important subject concepts toward which you should target your portfolio.

Once you have selected your course, carefully read the course description. This description is a key factor in determining how your portfolio

Find the course description and syllabus you need on the Web.

is evaluated. If you find several course descriptions for the same subject, choose the one that most closely reflects your learning.

Here are a few ways to find the courses you need:

PRINTED COLLEGE CATALOGS. Large libraries (especially college libraries) have collections of college catalogs; sometimes they're on microfiche.

ONLINE COLLEGE CATALOGS. Most colleges' Web sites list their course titles and descriptions online. Often you can review a course syllabus online too.

YOUR COLLEGE ADVISOR. Your advisor may be able to give you recommendations if the course you're considering is routinely taken by other students within your major.

PROFESSORS. A Web search might turn up several professors with special expertise in the subject you've learned. Some might be willing to help you find a course that fits your experience.

I struggled to find a course in international business ethics that matched my experience. After a lengthy and fruitless examination of college catalogs, I turned to the Web. However, all I found on the Internet was a list of organizations that conduct research in that field. Then I had an idea: *Why not*

The course description is a key factor in determining how your portfolio is evaluated.

e-mail these organizations and see if they can help me find a professor who teaches this subject? It worked! Before long, a professor had e-mailed me a course description, course syllabus, and even a list of recommended study resources. Wow! Everything I needed to create a winning portfolio!

STEP 3: *Make sure that the credit for the course you have selected fits into your degree program.*

Some schools have a more developed portfolio assessment program. They will assign a portfolio advisor who will guide you through the process of building your portfolio. Your advisor makes sure that the course you've chosen is compatible with your degree program and that your proposed portfolio will fulfill the requirements of the course. By working closely with my portfolio advisor through the entire process, I saved time and avoided potential errors.

STEP 4: *Describe your learning experience in a narrative.*

By working closely with my portfolio advisor through the entire process, I saved time and avoided potential errors.

Before developing your portfolio, attempt to contact your evaluator to find out what specific things he or she would like to see included. Not all evaluators use the same criteria.

Portfolio evaluators certainly want your narrative to tell what you learned through your experience, but they also want to know how you learned it. Your narrative should answer these questions:

- How did you do it?
- Where did your learning take place?
- When did your learning take place and how much time did you spend acquiring it?
- What depth of knowledge did you gain of the subject you studied?
- Who were the people involved in your learning experience?
- Why did you choose this kind of learning experience?

Course descriptions break down course content into the various subtopics that will be covered. For instance, a course called "Marriage and Family" might cover the subtopics of family lifecycles, problems within family relationships, and methods for studying family relationships. When you write your narrative, you must be sure to show that your experience covered each of these subtopics. This will be one of the most important criteria used in evaluating your portfolio.

There are two basic ways to organize a narrative: chronologically or topically. The chronological method is easier to write and may be preferred, provided each subtopic is addressed. Using the topical method makes it easier for an evaluator to tell if your narrative lacks strength in any one of the subtopics.

There are two basic ways to organize a narrative: chronologically or topically.

The quality of your writing is a critical factor in the success of your portfolio. By mastering the finer elements of grammar, usage, and style, you will be able to submit an outstanding report. In Chapter 12 we'll cover all the techniques you need for quick and effective writing.

Here are the six items that a good narrative should include.

1. **Describe your relevant learning experiences.** What did you actually do? This is an opportunity for you to describe the details of your experiences.

2. **Explain what you learned through these experiences.** Don't just tell what you did—clearly explain why these experiences were critical to your learning process.

3. **Describe specific points that are included to authenticate your learning experience.** Don't assume that the person evaluating your portfolio will instantly recognize the various points of learning that you have included in the portfolio.

4. **Explain your reasons for including each specific point.** How does the evidence you included support your claim for college credit? Everything you include in a portfolio should have a purpose. This is not a scrapbook!

The quality of your writing is a critical factor in the success of your portfolio.

5. **Demonstrate your understanding of the subject.** What are the major principles, theories, and terms related to the subject? Address each topic that you found in the course description.

6. **Explain why the knowledge that you have acquired is important to you.** How does what you have learned help you understand other subjects, help you in your work, or simply make you a better person? There should be a purpose for your learning. What is it?

STEP 5: Present evidence that documents and verifies your learning.

In your narrative, you addressed each topic stated in the course description and demonstrated your understanding of these areas. Next, authenticate the claims you have made about your learning. The evidence you include for a portfolio can be:

- samples of your work,
- official verification of attaining the required level of proficiency, or
- other documentation demonstrating your acquisition of knowledge.

*Everything
you include in a
portfolio should have
a purpose.*

These items might include:

- Course transcripts
- Annotated bibliography
- Official course description and syllabus
- Completed class assignments
- Certificates of completion
- Class notes
- Diploma
- Graded tests
- Reports
- Artwork
- Licenses

- Letters from supervisors or employees
- Work samples
- Performance evaluations
- Awards
- Newspaper and magazine clippings
- Mementos from countries lived in and visited
- Videotapes
- Photographs
- Programs from performances

As you can see, building a great portfolio is not very difficult when you use these five steps. To make it even easier, I've designed a portfolio worksheet for you to use; it's in Appendix D.

GETTING CREDIT

Upon completion of your portfolio, submit it to the evaluator as soon as possible. Since evaluation usually takes one to three months, plan ahead if you are faced with a deadline.

When you receive a passing grade for your portfolio, credit will be awarded and the transcript will include your portfolio work as simply another completed course. If the institution awarding the credit is not the college that will grant your degree, ask them to send the transcript to your college. This is usually a simple, inexpensive process.

QUESTIONS AND ANSWERS ON PORTFOLIO ANALYSIS

Are certain subjects inappropriate for portfolio assessment? Yes. Don't use portfolio assessment for subjects that are covered by standardized examinations, such as CLEP or DANTES. Also, physical education courses are generally not appropriate.

What courses are best suited to portfolio assessment? The answer to this question really depends upon your interests and your major. Ideally, you'll do portfolios for hard-to-find courses, advanced-level courses, and courses that are of particular interest to you. I did a portfolio for course work within my major's specialization because it was very interesting to me and I wanted

The Components of a Well Constructed Portfolio

① Cover Sheet

② List of Attachments
A.
B.
C.
D.

Your Portfolio

④ Evidence

③ Narrative

Letter

Ticket Ticket Ticket

Bibliography

Certificate ☆

. . . you end up with a collection of well-constructed portfolios that demonstrate how you mastered the subject through real-life experiences.

something documenting my real-life experiences and the knowledge I had gained in the field that I was entering.

If the school I'm planning on attending doesn't offer a program for portfolio assessment, can I still use this method for earning credit toward my degree? Yes. Some colleges have a special program that provides portfolio assessment for students that are not enrolled in their institution. If you obtain credit for your portfolio through one of these schools, you can then have the credits transferred to your college. I strongly recommend that you first check with your college to get prior approval for this type of credit transfer.

How long does it take to complete a portfolio? It could take from a few days to several months, depending on the nature of your portfolio. A portfolio for a course in basic oil painting might only involve writing a simple narrative, explaining the basic techniques, and gathering photographs of your

Since evaluation usually takes one to three months, plan ahead if you are faced with a deadline.

Thomas Edison is a leader in portfolio assessment.

work. The complexity of the subject, the nature of your experience, and how well you have documented your learning largely determine how much time and effort it will take to complete your portfolio.

Can I plan portfolios before I actually have the necessary experiences? Yes. Identify what you want to learn ahead of time and then develop a course of portfolio study. Course descriptions will help you determine what learning experiences you will need to have.

Can I get credit through portfolio assessment if I only have partial experience in a subject? Maybe! Sometimes through independent reading you can strengthen an area where your knowledge of the subject is deficient. When you're writing your narrative and come to a topic in which you don't have experience, you can refer to what you learned through your reading. Document your reading with an annotated bibliography and include it as a piece of evidence in the portfolio. An annotated bibliography is a list of book titles with a few sentences describing each book's major concepts as they relate to the focus of your portfolio.

How much does it cost to earn credit through portfolio assessment? Some schools let you pay a comprehensive tuition that covers the cost of any portfolio work you do through the school. Otherwise, the cost will be comparable to what you'd pay for a standard college course.

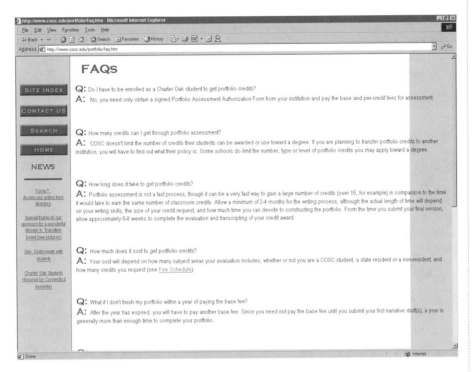

Charter Oak offers helpful answers to questions about portfolio assessment.

How much credit can be earned through portfolio assessment? It depends on your school. Some schools will accept only a few credits from portfolio assessment; others allow you to complete an entire degree through portfolios.

What are my chances of successfully getting credit through portfolio assessment? Some portfolio assessment programs claim their students have a 90 percent success rate in getting credit awarded for their portfolios. Follow the five steps I have outlined and you'll be successful too!

How many colleges offer programs for portfolio assessment? While only a handful of colleges offer well-developed, comprehensive programs for portfolio assessment, a growing number of colleges offer at least some options for earning portfolio credit, and most colleges accept transfer credit earned through portfolio assessment. For a complete list of colleges offering credit through portfolio assessment, see this book's companion volume, *The Accelerated Distance Learner's Guide to Colleges.*

How can I learn more about portfolio assessment? Schools that accept portfolios usually offer a handbook to guide you in building portfolios that are appropriate for assessment through their school. The following two colleges

A growing number of colleges offer at least some options for earning portfolio credit, and most colleges accept transfer credit earned through portfolio assessment.

have excellent portfolio assessment programs and have handbooks available for purchase.

Thomas Edison State College
(609) 984-1141
portfolio@call.tesc.edu
www.tesc.edu

Charter Oak State College
(860) 832-3800
info@mail.cosc.edu
www.cosc.edu

STUDENT'S POINT OF VIEW: *Using Portfolio Assessment to Qualify for a Teaching Position*
NAME: *Heidi Caasi*
HOME STATE: *Minnesota*
DEGREE: *Bachelor of Arts*
COLLEGE: *Thomas Edison*
AGE AT GRADUATION: 24

Portfolio assessment played a major role in the completion of my degree. Fifty percent of all the credits I earned were completed through this distance-learning method. The greatest benefit of portfolio assessment is its flexibility. Whenever I could find a topic in which I had knowledge or experience that matched a course description of some regionally accredited institution, I was able to prepare a portfolio that could be submitted for assessment. My home study of music harmony, unaccredited classroom experiences, attendance of several seminars, and travel in the Middle East all translated into bona fide credits on my college transcript.

I am very thankful for the wisdom that my father showed in encouraging me to earn my degree through distance learning. Six months after my marriage to my husband Ron, we were made legal guardians of his three nephews. We found it to be in the best interest of our new family for me to teach at a small Christian school in the same classroom as two of the boys. Without portfolio assessment, I would never have been able to quickly complete my degree, and I would not qualify for my current teaching position.

BEGIN BUILDING YOUR PORTFOLIOS!

Getting college credit through portfolio assessment is very rewarding. The process of getting the credit is fun and challenging, and when you're done, you really have something to show for your work! Imagine completing college, and rather than having a bunch of graded papers and examinations, you end up with a collection of well-constructed portfolios that demonstrate how you mastered the subject through real-life experiences. What a tremendous tool this would be in getting a job!

Internships:

College Credits That Will
Jump-Start Your Career

5

By now you're starting to see how quickly and conveniently you can earn your degree through Accelerated Distance Learning. Maybe you're wondering, "What am I going to do with all the extra time I'm saving?" Here's my advice: pursue real-life learning experiences through internships. Later, your internships may be a decisive factor in obtaining a job.

Internships were a major part of my education. I interned in landscaping, construction, government, missions, management consulting, education, and small business operation. These experiences took me from coast to coast and even around the world. More than any other educational experiences I have had, the internships helped me discover my life purpose. Looking back, I wouldn't trade those internships for any other learning experience, and certainly not for a series of classroom lectures!

Within the last few years, internships have grown tremendously in popularity. Now, almost 90% of students graduating from college have participated in at least one internship.

That's not surprising in light of current trends. Our society's transition to an information economy is forcing companies to develop innovative ways to provide their employees with continuing education and on-the-job training. Due to the shortage of competent labor, companies are increasingly leaning toward hiring and training interns. Internship opportunities have grown in number, scope, and worldwide availability and have become one of the best ways to become familiar with working in the international environment. Often, the internships you have completed will become your most outstanding and recognized credentials.

"An ounce of experience is worth a ton of theory." — Benjamin Franklin

Often, the internships you have completed will become your most outstanding and recognized credentials.

47

CHOOSING BETWEEN AN EXISTING INTERNSHIP PROGRAM OR DESIGNING YOUR OWN

If you can't find an opportunity that matches your needs, you should seriously consider designing your own internship.

In considering an internship, one of the first things you will have to decide is whether you should enter an existing internship program or develop one of your own. If you can't find an opportunity that matches your needs, you should seriously consider designing your own internship. The first thing to ask is, what areas of learning or work experience are of interest to you? Next, identify individuals and companies that specialize in those areas. Present an outline to your potential supervisor describing the type of experience that you hope to gain. Also, draw up a learning contract that specifies the terms of your internship—number of hours per week, scope of service, and nature of learning opportunities.

Usually there is a better chance of working out a satisfactory arrangement if you have a previous relationship with the individual or company that you have in mind. When I wanted to learn some construction skills, my father helped me approach a house builder in our church about the possibility of working for him for a few months. After we explained the type of experience I was seeking, we outlined a plan, and he agreed to it. Because we knew each other before the internship began, we quickly built a solid friendship. This gentleman took a special interest in me. He always took time to answer my questions and made sure I did a variety of tasks so that my experience was well rounded.

There are advantages and disadvantages to each internship method. Here is a quick comparison:

PREEXISTING vs. SELF-MADE INTERNSHIPS	
PREEXISTING	SELF-MADE
More structure	More flexibility
More exacting qualifications	Easier to qualify for
Usually the only method available for doing internships with large organizations	Usually the only method available for doing internships with small organizations
Opportunity to meet more experts	More meaningful mentoring relationships
More widely accepted	Less widely accepted
Tailored to the needs of the "average" student	Tailored to your specific needs
More focused learning experience	Broader learning experience

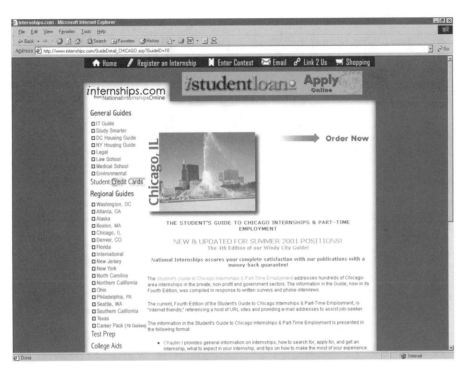

Looking for internships in Chicago? Check out internships.com for regional availability of internships.

ESTABLISHING CRITERIA FOR CHOOSING YOUR INTERNSHIP

There are thousands of internship opportunities—how will you know which one is right for you? The key is deciding in advance what are the most important issues to you and then finding an existing program or developing your own that matches the criteria you have established. Here are the main points to consider when determining what you want to learn from an internship experience:

- ELIGIBILITY. In the past, internships were available only to college students. Today, however, there are numerous opportunities for people of all ages and from all stages of life. Sometimes certain age, grade level, major, or GPA restrictions will apply.

- CENTERED ON LEARNING. While a certain amount of busywork is expected in most internships, it should not occupy most of your time. Don't give up your entire summer just to sort mail and answer phone calls! Make sure the internship is designed to provide you with real learning experiences.

The key is deciding in advance what are the most important issues to you and then finding an existing program or developing your own that matches the criteria you have established.

Carefully inquire what type of projects and learning opportunities will be available to you.

- FOCUSED ON YOUR AREA OF NEED. If you're interested in learning about computer networking, don't assume that an internship at Microsoft will automatically guarantee this type of learning experience. Carefully inquire what type of projects and learning opportunities will be available to you. If the internship won't allow you to learn what you need, look elsewhere.

- OPPORTUNITY FOR MENTORING RELATIONSHIPS. One outstanding aspect of internships is the opportunity to be mentored by someone already possessing the specific skills and knowledge you need. These relationships made a very deep, lasting impact on my life. My mentors taught me valuable skills, but more importantly, they helped me develop a vision for what I wanted to do with my life.

- OPPORTUNITY FOR NETWORKING. Good internships allow you to meet new people and form beneficial relationships. If carefully chosen, these relationships can last much longer and become more important than the initial internship experience. When I did an internship in small business management under one of my father's friends, I was able to interact with him on both a professional and personal level. He has become a trusted business advisor and counselor for my life.

- ACCOMMODATIONS. This could mean the difference between a great internship and an unbearable one. Sometimes established internship programs include housing for interns—but be forewarned, it might not be like your parents' home!

- OPPORTUNITY FOR FUTURE EMPLOYMENT. Often, the first place a company will turn to when they have a job opening is their pool of past and present interns. Do you want to scout out a particular job position and see if it has potential for you? Become an intern with the company. It's a great way to test the waters.

- COMPENSATION. Some companies actually pay their interns very generously. While compensation should not be your sole motivation for doing an internship, it is an important consideration.

- INTERNATIONAL COMPONENT. Does the internship allow you to gain some sort of international experience? Will it require you to live or work in another country? This type of internship is especially valuable. In addition to your formal duties as an intern, you will have the opportunity to learn about the language and culture of

Principle #6: GLOBAL PERSPECTIVE. The revolution that has taken place in the world's information and communication systems requires that we develop a global perspective on life.

another part of the world. In today's global economy, this kind of experience is far more important than you may realize.

THE APPLICATION PROCESS

Once you have identified which internships interest you, it's time to start applying. The application format will depend on the specific opportunity you choose. You might need to write a letter stating why you are interested in the internship, send in a résumé, and/or provide a transcript that shows your GPA.

Before submitting your application, learn as much as possible about the business, discovering exactly what they do. In your application, reflect this information and your own enthusiasm about the opportunity to serve with such an outstanding company. Companies want interns who understand their business and are excited about the opportunity to learn more.

Getting College Credit for Your Internship Experience

In the past, although internships added to your academic experience, they did not result in credits toward a college degree. With portfolio assessment now being more widely recognized, you can receive the real-life experience of an internship and college credit too. There are two ways to do this:

1. CREDIT EQUIVALENCY. You may be able to find a college that already offers credit for the internship you plan to take. Even if you aren't enrolled in that college, this is still good news. Because the internship is already academically recognized and a course description exists for it, demonstrating its academic worth in your portfolio will be easier. Getting credit might be as simple as sending your school a copy of the course description from the school granting credit for the internship and a letter of successful internship completion from the program director. Many schools handle these papers like a transcript and award credit accordingly.

2. DOCUMENT AS YOU GO. Even if you are unable to find a college that currently offers credit for your internship experience, there are still ways to get credit for it. Find a course that covers the knowledge you have gained from your experience and then use it for your portfolio. For example, if you completed an internship at your state capitol, one of the colleges in your area probably offers courses on state and local government. Take that course description and write a narrative based on your internship experience that describes your equivalent knowledge of the major subjects

Companies want interns who understand their business and are excited about the opportunity to learn more.

taught within that course. The key to successful portfolios is documenting as you go. Here's how:

- FIND A COURSE DESCRIPTION. If possible, do this even before beginning the internship experience. The course description will help focus your internship on key areas of learning.

- KEEP A "LEARNING JOURNAL." A learning journal allows you to document your learning experiences every day so you will be able to write an accurate narrative about what you learned.

- SAVE WORK PROJECTS. What did you do in your internship? Copy documents that you helped produce. For large items, take pictures documenting your work.

- GET LETTERS. Have the director of the internship program, your immediate supervisor, and others with whom you worked provide letters outlining the dates and duration of your internship, the scope of your responsibilities, and additional information about the internship.

- TAKE TESTS. The program administrator may be able to test you on some aspect of the learning experience. A scored test sheet can serve as evidence for your portfolio.

- GET FEEDBACK. Establish regular times to talk with your supervisor/mentor, during which you ask questions or make comments about what you have learned. Get feedback from your mentor on what you should be learning. This will enrich and direct your learning experience. Don't forget to record notes from these meetings and document what you are learning.

FINDING THE PERFECT INTERNSHIP EXPERIENCE

Finding the right internship experience is a lot easier when you have the right tools. These Web sites contain information and searchable databases of internships available throughout the world:

Internship Search Engine
www.internshipprograms.com
Using this online database you can search for internship opportunities by location or company name. It also contains many helpful student reviews.

Student Advantage

www.studentadvantage.com

This site's "Internships/Co-ops" section contains many articles written by students on topics related to internship programs.

Job Monkey

www.jobmonkey.com

Job Monkey's mission is to "help you find seasonal or year-round jobs working for employers who can offer unique opportunities to travel the world, have fun, and earn good money doing it."

Student.com

www.student.com/subsection/summerjobs

Contains good reviews written by students who participated in a variety of internship opportunities.

Peterson's Internships 2006 describes more than 50,000 internship opportunities and is a great place to start your search. See the *Student Success Catalog* for more information.

Taking Online and Correspondence Courses:

6

College Classes Beyond the Four Walls

The number of students taking online courses exploded by an estimated 70 percent from 1997 to 1998. Today more than a million students are taking courses online, and many more are using other correspondence methods. Students enjoy this method of distance learning because it provides structured learning and the opportunity to study under the guidance of a professor. Yet, at the same time, online courses offer flexible and creative learning experiences.

SELECTING YOUR COURSES

With distance learning and online education, you have choices that your parents would never have even dreamed about. This is certainly exciting, but it also creates a great challenge before you in discerning which course opportunity to pursue. Before registering for a course, make sure that you have carefully thought through the following questions.

How does this course fit into my overall degree program? The student counseling or advising department of your school will help you find out if the course you have chosen is appropriate for your degree as well as answer your questions regarding any other aspect of your degree-completion process. Schools vary in how they classify courses. As I was preparing to take a course in business ethics, I discovered that although the school that offered the course classified it as a business course (which was compatible with my major), the school to which I was transferring the credit classified it as a philosophy course, and therefore it did not fit into my degree program. Watch out for these incompatibilities.

Online courses offer flexible and creative learning experiences.

STUDENT'S POINT OF VIEW: *Tips for Success in Correspondence Courses*

NAME: *Andrew Cope*
HOME STATE: *South Carolina*
MAJOR: *Bachelor of General Studies*
COLLEGE: *Indiana University*
AGE AT GRADUATION: *Currently enrolled*
CURRENT AGE: *23*

Taking correspondence courses has been rewarding for me as a student; yet, in my experience, I have found them to be more intensive than traditional classroom courses. On the other hand, the flexibility inherent in this method of learning has allowed me to work on courses when and where my schedule dictates.

One thing to keep in mind when taking courses by correspondence is the time factor. The overall amount of time required to complete the course will be affected by the grade that you feel you need to achieve. Spending more time on assignments will usually result in a higher grade, but this time must be balanced with your overall goal for completing the degree. Also, different instructors will grade assignments in different ways. For instance, some professors merely prefer excellence in grammar, while others demand it. Again, the student has to constantly balance his or her efforts with their schedule for course completion.

Personally, I would not recommend taking more than two courses at a time. With fewer courses, you can maximize your study time. If you have to relearn any material because you stopped to work on another course, the overall time required for both courses will be increased. Conversely, I do prefer to stay enrolled in two courses at a time because it eliminates delays associated with the correspondence medium.

Lastly, the most important skill for working through correspondence is writing. Writing concisely, clearly, and quickly are mandatory abilities to this method of learning, and this skill should be honed before attempting upper-level courses that are more writing-intensive. Of all the skills I have learned via my college work, I feel that writing has been the most beneficial. God has given me a vision for serving him in the business world, and effective documentation and communication remain essential skills in that arena.

Be sure to find out if the course you are taking is accredited if you plan to transfer it to an accredited college.

Is the course accredited and how will it transfer to my school? Be sure to find out if the course you are taking is accredited, if you plan to transfer it to an accredited college. For more information on this important issue, see Chapter 14. If the course is accredited and you have permission from your college to use it for earning credit toward your degree, you shouldn't have any problems getting your credits transferred. Schools vary in how they handle this process, but most colleges will be able to seamlessly transfer the credit from their college to yours.

Will I be able to take the course on an accelerated basis? Once you begin applying the techniques shared in Part III, you will be learning faster than you ever dreamed possible. As a result, you will probably want to take some of your online and correspondence courses on an accelerated basis. This means shortening the traditional 16-week semester down to whatever amount of time works best for you—maybe only a few weeks.

Most schools give you a fair amount of flexibility in completing your course work, and some allow you to accelerate the course. If you want to accelerate a course, you should first send a written letter of request to your college's registrar, explaining your reasons for wanting to accelerate the course. If your request is accepted, the second thing you will need to do is notify the professor who will be grading your tests and other assignments. Give notice that you will be submitting these early. The third thing you might have to do is contact the college's testing center and request that your tests be mailed out early to the testing lab that you plan to use. Once these details are handled, you'll be ready to fly through these courses with amazing speed.

Will I be able to devote the required amount of time to completing the course? Not every online course requires the same amount of time and involvement. Find out how many and what type of assignments will be involved, what resources will be used, and whether instruction will be totally flexible or delivered according to a specific schedule. Most schools encourage you to plan approximately 9–15 hours a week for 16 weeks to complete a 3-credit-hour course. Remember though, by using the accelerated learning techniques in the next section of the book, you'll be able to learn at a much faster pace. I usually completed my courses in less than one-fourth of the standard time.

How does the course content compare with similar courses that you could take instead? You'll often find that although two courses are named the same, they can differ greatly in their content. Determine what you want to focus on in your studies and pick the course that meets your needs.

Who will be the professor and what kind of teaching style does he/she have? In the world of online education, you are the one who chooses your professors, so choose wisely. Try to pick professors who will make their courses student-directed and student-centered. This means that the teacher's focus is not on teaching, but rather on helping you learn. Sometimes

"Good things when short are twice as good." — Baltasar Gracian

I usually completed my courses in less than one-fourth of the standard time.

you can discover a great deal about your professors from their personal Web pages or their school's Web site.

Are there prerequisites for the course? Most upper-level (300–400) courses require that you first complete one or more prerequisite courses. These prerequisite courses will ensure that you maintain higher academic performance on the upper-level courses.

What will be the medium of instruction? With a multitude of learning formats available through online education, try to choose one that's suited to your needs. Do you find audio instruction too difficult to follow? Then avoid courses that rely heavily on recorded lectures. Are you a visual learner? Courses that incorporate multimedia instruction will probably be a better choice for you.

Does the course require facilities and equipment that I can easily access? Some courses require testing in a specialized computer-testing lab, which may not be available in your area. Other courses may require that you have certain multimedia or videoconferencing tools on your computer.

COMPARING COURSE COSTS

Generally, online courses don't cost any less than classroom courses. However, if you shop around, you may be able to find some real bargains. The basic cost of any course is the cost per credit multiplied by the number of credits for the course. In addition to your basic tuition, you may have to pay one or more of the following surcharges for online courses:

TECHNOLOGY FEE OR TELECOMMUNICATIONS CHARGE. This fee covers the cost of the telecommunications services that the school must use in order to provide you with online courses.

NONRESIDENT CHARGE. State colleges usually offer one price to residents and another price to nonresident students. This pricing policy can often double the price of a college course if you are a nonresident. So watch out for it.

MAILING CHARGE. How will you return completed tests and assignments to your professors? Schools differ in their policies. When I took courses from Thomas Edison, I paid about $3.60 per course for postage.

TEXTBOOKS. The cost of books for your course can be as much as $100 per course. On the other hand, if you can use Web-based instructional tools or obtain required materials through your library, you may not have to spend a dime on books.

If you shop around, you may be able to find some real bargains.

VIDEOS AND TAPES. Some courses require you to purchase or rent audio-visual materials. These could cost you $20 to $100. Since these materials require an extra expense and because they take longer to work through, I usually chose to stick with textbooks.

COURSE EXTENSION FEE. Once you start applying the accelerated learning methods in Part III, I doubt you'll need to pay this fee. If you do need a longer period of time than the standard 16-week semester, plan on paying from $50 to $100 for permission to extend the deadline for your course.

CREDIT TRANSFER FEE. After finishing the course, you may have to pay a fee to have the accumulated credit transferred to another school. Most colleges can send a transcript that lists all of your completed courses and grades for a charge of $3 to $15.

CREDENTIAL EVALUATION FEE. Credits that you have transferred to another college may incur various extra fees as the courses are evaluated, accepted, and finally transferred as credit to a cumulative transcript.

For more information on the costs of distance-learning education and how to pay for it, see Chapter 15.

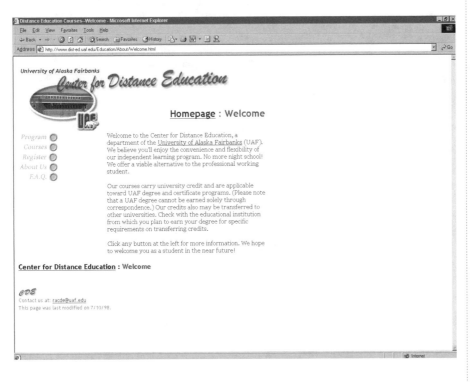

Find out more about course format and delivery methods by going directly to the home pages of college distance-learning departments.

REGISTERING FOR YOUR COURSES

Work out a long-term plan for your studies and get it approved by your advisor. This will help balance your course load and ensure that you don't miss deadlines. Most schools consider 12 to 15 credits of course work per semester a full course load, but a focused student can usually take on more. Your school might limit the number of credit hours for which you can register at their school each semester, but this doesn't mean you can't simultaneously take courses from another school. After completing the course, simply have the credits transferred to your school.

Like classroom courses, online courses have registration deadlines. Plan to register at least one month in advance. Not only should this ensure that you get into the course before it fills up, but some schools offer significant discounts for early registration.

Most schools allow you to register by mail, telephone, fax, or computer. I generally prefer online registration because it is fast, avoids having to wait on hold, and provides all of the information in one place so I can make an

Register for courses online.

informed decision. It's also the most dependable, avoiding any communication errors that sometimes occur when using other methods of registration.

THE COURSE WORK ITSELF

Most course work typically consists of a number of written assignments, research projects, and exams.

The courses I took each required the completion of six written papers and two exams—a midterm and a final. Six papers might sound like a lot of work, but it wasn't really too bad. Although I was required to write four to seven pages per paper, much of that was a summary of what I had learned from the assigned readings.

In my own experience, the content of the exams I took was very focused on the texts that I was given to study—I didn't encounter any surprise questions about things that were not covered.

Most courses include some type of syllabus that will help identify the most important concepts in the course and assist you in staying on schedule.

Correspondence courses typically require more reading than classroom-based courses. However, by using speed-reading techniques like those we'll discuss in Chapter 10, you'll be able to cruise through a course in less time than its classroom-based counterpart. Learning textual information is always much faster using speed-reading techniques than listening to lectures.

COMMUNICATE!

Successful students must be willing and able to communicate. The more you communicate, the more effective and smooth your learning process will be. Just because you are learning at a distance should not mean that you're out of touch with what's happening. In fact, successful distance-learning students generally experience more meaningful interaction than their classroom counterparts.

As a distance learner you'll need to communicate with:

PROFESSORS. Don't hesitate to ask for additional help or clarification of assignments. Most professors teaching distance-learning courses realize that they have a greater responsibility to be available to their students and facilitate two-way communication. The feedback that you provide also helps them to know how to teach distance courses more effectively. Many distance-learning students feel that they actually receive more individualized attention from professors than they would in a classroom setting.

Tip: Before you begin any of your studies, make it your goal to master speed-reading skills.

Correspondence courses typically require more reading than classroom-based courses.

The more you communicate, the more effective and smooth your learning process will be.

Many distance-learning students feel that they actually receive more individualized attention from professors than they would in a classroom setting.

FELLOW STUDENTS. You're not the only one taking the course. Talking to other students about what they've learned from the course can greatly enrich your own understanding. Because online courses have the potential to connect you with a global student community, you can benefit from the rich variety of perspectives and experiences of an international student body.

EXPERTS. In addition to your assigned professor, who are the experts in the subject you are studying? Who are the researchers working on the cutting edge of developments within the subject? Who are the business people that deal with the issues on a practical day-to-day basis? The Internet can assist you first in finding out who these people are and then linking you up with them so you are able to communicate and glean from their expertise.

COLLEGE STAFF AND ADVISORS. After your course work is finished, make sure your college has received and recorded all grades, credits, and transcripts. Request that an official transcript of your college work be mailed to you.

DISTANCE-LEARNING TECHNOLOGIES

Two basic types of communication technologies are used in distance learning, *synchronous* and *asynchronous*. During asynchronous communi-

Check assignments and schedules online.

cation there is a time lapse between the teacher's instruction and the student's learning. The teacher produces the instructional materials and sends them to the students. After learning the material and completing the assignments, the student returns them to the teacher who then assigns a grade. The downside to asynchronous communication is having to wait. The advantage is that you are completely free to study at your own pace.

With synchronous communication, the teaching and learning take place at the same time, normally through videoconferencing and other computer-assisted technologies. This form of instruction is more interactive and can be interesting, but you *must* get to class on time!

Here's an overview of the technologies you may need to use in order to complete online courses.

PRINT. Regardless of the type of distance-learning course you choose, to some extent, it will make use of the oldest of all distance-learning technologies—simple print. How you deal with the print that you receive may differ depending on how it is formatted. While printed books will generally require you to move in a steady line from front to back, the print in a hypertext Web document can be maneuvered from many directions and allows you to easily focus on the parts that interest you most.

VIDEO. Obviously, the benefit of video-based instruction is that it allows you to see the information presented graphically. The downside is the cost (you must rent or purchase the tapes) and the time required. Personally, I learn much faster when I'm reading, so I would tend to avoid video instruction. However, you might find that this method works well for you.

AUDIO. Unlike videotapes, audio presentations can be an efficient way to learn because you can do other things while you listen. These audio classes might include prerecorded lectures or even live broadcasts which you can hear through your college's Web site. Many schools still offer audio-based instruction by sending audiocassettes in the mail. However, unless you are an auditory learner, you should probably stay away from courses that rely heavily on this medium of instruction.

VIDEOCONFERENCING. Normal video-based instruction is only one-way, but videoconferencing allows you to engage in two-way, real-time communication with full motion, full-color video, and audio. Using this technology, students from virtually anywhere on the globe can meet face to face.

With **facilities-based videoconferencing**, students meet at a remote learning site established by the school to listen to lectures and engage in

"The man who goes alone can start today; but he who travels with another must wait till that other is ready."
—Henry David Thoreau

discussions monitored by a professor at another site. Facilities-based videoconferencing is less flexible than desktop-based and carries many of the drawbacks associated with traditional classroom teaching. **Desktop-based**

FROM THE EXPERT: *Audioconferencing Technology Expands Distance Learning Opportunities*

NAME: *Ronald D. Illingworth*
POSITION: *Academic Program Head*
DEPARTMENT: *Center for Distance Education*
SCHOOL: *University of Alaska, Fairbanks*

Audioconference courses are courses which closely approximate traditional face-to-face courses but which are accomplished at a distance. In an audioconferenced course, the students and the instructor all call in to a toll-free number at a specific time. For example, my "Literature of Alaska and the Yukon" class meets every Tuesday and Thursday evening from 8:30 to 9:45 Alaska time. The students and I become a "community on the phone," just as if we were all in the same location. In a manner similar to a face-to-face class, students have an opportunity to interact with their classmates and with the instructor. At the same time, the instructor has the opportunity to conduct short lectures, moderate discussions, and conduct short oral quizzes. Additionally, students may present materials and reports. All that is necessary for physical equipment is a telephone. A speakerphone with a mute button is advantageous, but is not a necessity. Students feel very comfortable using the telephone since they are all familiar with it.

Most courses can be taught using the audioconference system. We teach literature courses, lab science courses, math courses, history courses, nursing courses, and teacher education courses to name just a few. We have not attempted to deliver upper-division lab science courses because of the highly specialized lab equipment components that are necessary. Similarly, intensively hands-on courses such as welding have not been attempted by audioconference.

We offer approximately eighty-five audioconferenced courses each semester to over 1,000 students throughout rural Alaska. For most of these students, the audioconference is the only way they have access to a post-secondary education. Currently, we are supplementing many of our audioconference courses with a Web component, adding a visual component to the instructional mix. One of the advantages to the audioconference course is the interaction students have with faculty and with other students in the course. This is generally impossible in correspondence courses and somewhat limited and restricted in Web-based courses.

videoconferencing allows individuals to connect using their own computers equipped with small video cameras ("Web cams").

For more in-depth information about videoconferencing, visit www.videoconference.com.

Multimedia. Whether via the Web, CD-ROM, or DVD, multimedia instruction can greatly enhance your learning experience. Cybercasts with instructors delivering lectures live over the Web; animations that simulate abstract or difficult information; tools such as specialized spreadsheets, calculators, and graphs; and graphics that visually represent information are just a sampling of what's available online. The quality of this instructional medium is improving constantly.

E-mail. You'll quickly discover that e-mail is non-optional. You'll use it to communicate with professors, advisors, and classmates. Some courses even allow you to submit assignments via e-mail. By attaching files to your e-mails you can easily send formatted documents, graphics, sound, and even video clips to others. If you need to send a document that is longer than one page, send it as an attached word processor document that can be easily printed for offline reading.

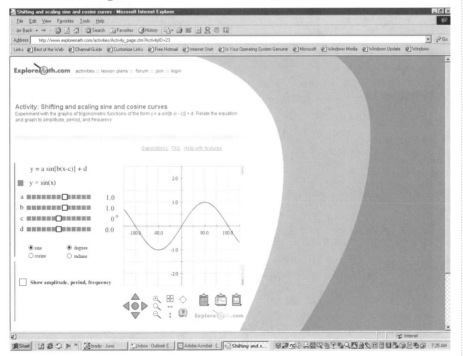

You'll quickly discover that e-mail is non-optional.

Orderly communication is facilitated by preset guidelines such as starting time, length, and subject matter of the chat session, who is allowed to participate, and who will moderate.

Interactive learning tools enhance the learning experience.

Sometimes professors will set up special password-protected bul-letin boards available only to their students for discussion of class content.

BULLETIN BOARDS. Electronic bulletin boards at most colleges are usually accessed through school Web sites. They provide a convenient place for students and faculty to engage in academic discussion. These discussions are arranged in "threads": strings of messages that are arranged by topic in such a way that they form a conversation. You can join an ongoing thread or start a new thread by asking a question or soliciting comments from others about a new topic. Sometimes professors will set up special password-protected bulletin boards available only to their students for discussion of class content. This provides a great way for classes to interact online without interruption.

INTERNET CHAT. An Internet chat is a live conversation via typed text messages. Your college may have a chat area on their Web site. Sometimes chat rooms are established for a class of distance-learning students to engage in formal class discussions led by an instructor. Other times they are simply a way for students to get together and talk. Orderly communication is facilitated by preset guidelines such as starting time, length, and subject matter of the chat session, who is allowed to participate, and who will moderate. While chatting can be interesting, remember that chatting can also be very

PURPOSEFUL DISCUSSIONS

Online discussion groups can be one of the best ways to communicate with classmates and professors. They can benefit your learning by:

- Integrating what you are learning.
- Clarifying your thinking on the subject.
- Stimulating further study and research.
- Giving an opportunity to practice communicating with others on the subject.
- Encouraging the development of collaborative problem-solving skills.
- Providing a sense of camaraderie and support.

A well-organized discussion group can deliver all these benefits in a very timely manner. Because conversation is limited to the subject material, time isn't wasted on small talk. When the discussion is complete, you have a handy copy of all your previous communication for future reference.

Discussion groups can be started by your school, professor, an outside organization, or even you!

When the discussion is complete, you have a handy copy of all your previous communication for future reference.

time-consuming and is generally less profitable than other distance-learning technologies.

READY TO TAKE YOUR FIRST CORRESPONDENCE COURSE?

Knowing how to take an online or correspondence course is something you'll find incredibly valuable, even after you get your degree. The information age will require workers to continually upgrade their skills, and correspondence courses will pave the way.

Independent Study and Community Colleges: 7

Local Resources for Distance Learners

Have you ever wondered how one teacher can meet the individual needs of thirty students and ensure that each has a positive learning experience? This goal is rarely achieved because the classroom model of teaching just doesn't lend itself to individual learning styles and student needs. What's the solution? Guided study. Guided study allows you to work one on one with a professor in completing a course. This individualized attention ensures that your learning experience will meet your real needs.

Guided study allows you to work one-on-one with a professor in completing a course.

A STUDY METHOD I HEARTILY RECOMMEND!

While I was earning my degree, I needed a course in export/import traffic management to meet a requirement in my degree specialization. I knew portfolio assessment wouldn't work for me because I lacked the experience. Online courses weren't available, and enrolling in a traditional course would consume too much time. Then I learned about guided study. I immediately began calling professors in my area that taught this course to see if one of them would do a guided study with me. After a couple of phone calls, I located a willing professor at my local community college.

During the course of several weeks, we met at times and locations convenient for both of us. At each meeting she would explain some of the more confusing or difficult concepts. Then she'd give me assignments structured to emphasize the Asian aspects of import/export business, since she knew I was preparing for future work in China. Because the course had practical application for me, I really enjoyed it.

Following a few weeks of enjoyable study, I received five credits and an "A" for the course. I filled out a simple form, paid an additional $3 transcript fee, and my credits were transferred to my college. "Wow," I thought. "If only more students knew how to do guided studies!"

The benefits of guided study include:

- Personal attention from a professor.
- Flexible timing for course completion.
- Courses tailored to meet your specific needs.

THREE KEYS FOR SUCCESSFUL GUIDED STUDIES

Key #1: Must be student-initiated.

While setting up a guided study may take a little more effort on your part than taking a standard course, the initial effort can really pay off. Colleges differ somewhat in their procedures for setting up independent studies, but generally, here's how it works:

Principle # 8: CUSTOMIZED LEARNING. Education should be customized to your learning style and needs.

1. **Find the course.** Determine what subject you need to study and then try to find a college in your area which offers that course. You might start your search by obtaining the catalogs of a few colleges in your area, or you could try finding the information online. Pay attention—colleges may use different names for the same subject. Once you have found a college offering the course, find out how to contact the program director or the professor who teaches it.

2. **Make inquiry.** Find out if the professor will allow you to do an independent study for the course rather than completing the normal course work. You might need to explain what you mean by "independent study" because some professors are not familiar with it. Once the instructor understands what you mean and why you want to do it this way—the flexibility, quality of learning, and course availability—there's a good chance they will give it a try. A key factor in receiving a positive response will be your own communication skills. When you approach a professor, be respectful and courteous. Manners still go a long way in opening many doors of opportunity.

Manners still go a long way in opening many doors of opportunity.

3. **Register.** Once you get the green light, you should find out how to sign up for the course and make your payment.

4. **Make your first appointment.** Contact the professor to set up the time and place for your first meeting.

Key #2: Must be student-directed.

During your first meeting, explain your purposes for taking the course. The professor might not be willing to change the content of the course for you, but may demonstrate flexibility in structuring assignments so they reflect your interests. You should know the answers to the following questions beforehand:

- What specific subjects within the course are especially interesting to me?
- Do I want to study these specific topics in greater depth?
- What part of the course will require greater assistance from the professor in order for me to clearly understand it?
- How does this course fit in with my other studies?
- How will the content of this course help me with my future work and goals?

Knowing the answers to these questions ahead of time and being able to clearly explain them to your professor will make a major difference in the quality of your learning experience. Throughout the entire course, consider yourself the *director* of your learning experience and your professor as its *facilitator*. This means you should actively ask questions and make sure what you are learning is in line with the goals you have established for the course.

Key #3: Must be student-responsible.

In an independent study, you are responsible to set up your meetings, complete assignments, and really learn what's important to you. The grade you receive in your independent study will be based on your character as well as your academic performance. When meeting with your professor, be punctual, dress sharp, and show genuine interest and enthusiasm about the subject.

When you finish the course, fill out a request for early grades (if needed) and then request that transcripts be sent to your college right away. While these may seem like minor details—you need to follow up on them.

Throughout the entire course, consider yourself the director of your learning experience and your professor as its facilitator.

When meeting with your professor, be punctual, dress sharp, and show genuine interest and enthusiasm about the subject.

The home page of a local community college.

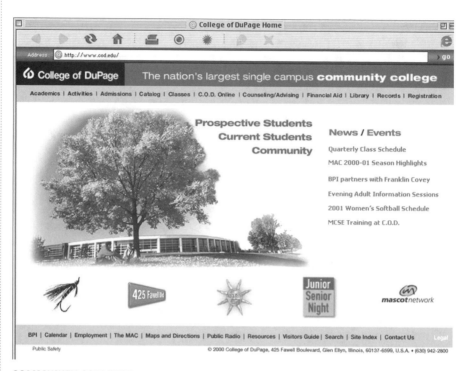

COMMUNITY COLLEGES

Although you are engaging in distance learning, don't overlook local resources that might be of help to you. One of the best local resources is your county or district community college. Community colleges, sometimes called junior colleges, are two-year schools that were established to make college education more accessible and affordable for local residents. Because of this, community colleges are fairly innovative in how they deliver educational services to the public. It is projected that an estimated 83 percent of U.S. community colleges will offer online courses by the year 2002. This is a good sign! It indicates that they are beginning to understand the needs of distance-learning students.

Faculty members at your local community college will usually be more eager to help you set up independent studies if they know the courses will contribute towards your degree completion.

Libraries

Check the community college library for the books and articles you need in order to conduct research for your course work. As with public libraries,

STUDENT'S POINT OF VIEW: *Flexibility at the Local Community College*

NAME: *David Beroth*
HOME STATE: *Ohio*
MAJOR: *Bachelor of Science in Business Administration, Accounting*
COLLEGE: *Thomas Edison State College*
AGE AT GRADUATION: *21*

    Local junior, technical, and community colleges are great resources for distance-learning students. I took quite a few courses through my local technical college that I later transferred to the distance-learning program from which I graduated. Rather than using my local technical college for general education classes like many students do, I used credit-by-examination programs such as CLEP to earn the lower-level credits and the technical college to complete courses in the area of my major.

    My local technical college was very flexible in accommodating my needs as a distance learner. For example, after enrolling in one of my advanced accounting courses, I realized that I had already acquired much of the knowledge presented in the course through my prior studies. So, after the class, I asked the instructor if I could simply take the final exam to earn the necessary credit. He agreed, and I passed. The other classroom courses I took were convenient, cost effective, and easily transferred to the college from which I graduated.

    Most important, though, was not the degree, but the pursuit of God's plan for my life. The credential I earned through distance learning has allowed me to join an accounting firm and serve in a worldwide missions organization using my professional skills.

Community college libraries are well equipped—best of all, they're free!

Proctored exams, unlike classroom exams, minimize distractions in the room and allow for flexible schedules.

district residents can borrow books and study them at home. Often, these libraries also provide computer workstations with Internet access. And, best of all, these services are usually free for community residents.

Examination Proctoring

Most community colleges have a testing lab that can proctor exams. Proctored exams, unlike classroom exams, minimize distractions in the room and allow for flexible schedules. These services are usually free to district residents. Contact the testing lab staff either in person or by phone and explain that you are pursuing your degree through distance study. Fill out a proctor request form authorizing the testing lab to administer your exams and then fax or mail this form to your college. When you're ready to take an exam, ask your college to send the test to the community college testing lab. You'll then be ready to take the test at the time you scheduled with the lab staff.

Courses

Sometimes, there is no difference in the content or requirements of a 200-level course offered by a community college and a 400-level course offered by a university.

The average community college offers a wide variety of courses that are often provided through non-traditional means. These 100- and 200-level courses are generally comparable to the courses taken during the first and second years of study toward a four-year bachelor's degree. While these courses are called entry-level courses, the content may vary in depth and specialization, depending on the course. Sometimes, there is no difference in the content or requirements of a 200-level course offered by a community college and a 400-level course offered by a university. Nonetheless, a uni-

Local testing labs help make testing convenient.

versity might not accept the 200-level community college course in lieu of the 400-level university course with comparable content. Don't start taking a community college course until you find out if the college you plan on graduating from will accept it toward your degree program.

Costs

State and local tax revenues help keep community colleges very affordable for local residents. When living in the Chicago area, I paid only $42 per credit. In Southern California, the cost is an unbelievably low $8 per credit. Sometimes it is possible to take advantage of the course offerings and discounts of several community colleges in your area. Incorporating community college courses into your degree plan is definitely a great way to minimize your tuition bill.

Credit Transfer

Not surprisingly, community colleges are very experienced at helping students transfer credits to other colleges. In most cases, the completed course will be recorded on your transcript in the same way a traditional course would be, regardless of how the credit was earned (e.g., credit-by-

Incorporating community college courses into your degree plan is definitely a great way to minimize your tuition bill.

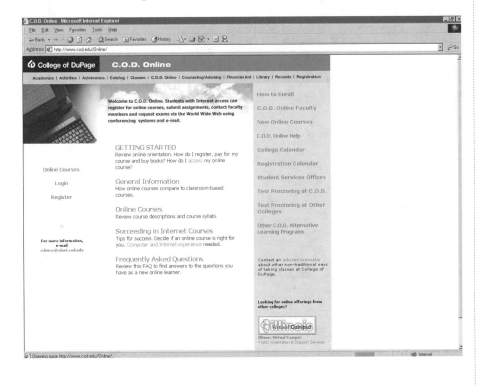

Alternative methods for earning credit through community colleges abound.

FROM THE EXPERT: *Community Colleges—Adapting to the Changing Communities They Serve*

NAME: *Ronald J. Schiesz*
POSITION: *Professor*
DEPARTMENT: *Independent Learning Center*
SCHOOL: *College of DuPage, Glen Ellyn, IL*

Community colleges have always prided themselves on how well they adapt to the changing needs of the community they serve. The challenge of using shrinking budgets to serve increasing numbers of students has caused community colleges to turn to technology to become more efficient and effective. As a result, higher and continuing education has become much more accessible, allowing learning in any place and at any time via the Internet and portable multimedia systems.

The Internet also allows community colleges to share resources for course development and faculty teaching through cooperative agreements and partnerships. This results in even more learning options and points of access for students. However, there is still much work to do. Contractual arrangements with faculty and among partnering community colleges are still being worked out, and research, comparing the quality of learning among these new formats, is still being performed.

Here at the Centers for Independent Learning at the College of DuPage, approximately 5,000 distance learners enroll for each 11-week academic quarter. The total enrollment at the college is approximately 34,000 each academic term. The flagship center on our main campus is a 16,000-square-foot facility specifically dedicated to serving distance learners with communications technology. We also have four satellite centers strategically located throughout the community. All of the community-based centers have open computer labs, private and group conferencing areas to meet with faculty, computer-based testing facilities, and distribution areas for multimedia checkout. The college's campus-wide fiber optic network allows students, faculty, and staff to electronically connect to the college. The centers offer 175 different independent study courses through various non-traditional formats including audio, video, local cable broadcasts, radio, and Internet. Subject areas range from developmental skills courses to general education, computer, and business-related college courses. All of these courses are equivalent in content to the classroom-based version of the course. About 170 faculty members instruct through the five Centers for Independent Learning.

Once thought of as peripheral and avant-garde, distance-learning technology is increasingly considered essential and fundamental for colleges and universities. Community colleges in general and the College of DuPage in particular have faced this challenge by using communications technology to provide the community access to instruction and services at a convenient pace, time, and location.

examination, portfolio assessment, online, or guided studies). In most cases, your college will accept or reject your transfer credits based solely on your final grade. To get the credits transferred you'll usually pay a small fee and fill out a simple form.

Why aren't community colleges more widely used?

By now you might be saying, "If community colleges have so much to offer, why don't more students take advantage of them?" Actually, many do. In recent years, 45 percent of all college students enrolled for classes in a community college. Most students know something about the traditional course work through community colleges but very little about the resources they make available for distance-learning students.

WHAT ARE YOU WAITING FOR?

Guided studies and community colleges provide wonderful opportunities to approach your studies with creativity and initiative. Call the community colleges in your area and order their course catalogs. Soon, you'll discover a multitude of exciting, tailor-made learning opportunities.

Online Study Resources:

Finding Your Way Through the Jungle

N ow that you've been introduced to distance-learning methods, it's time to start trekking through the jungle of the World Wide Web. Although adventure abounds in this exotic place, danger also lurks here. Because the Web is such a vast network of knowledge, it's easy to get distracted from your search and end up lost in cyberspace.

"The next best thing to knowing something is knowing where to find it." —Dr. Johnson

Here are a few pointers to help you stay on the trail:

- BE AN EARLY BIRD: Do your online research early in the morning when there is less Internet traffic.

- BEGIN WITH THE END IN MIND: Have a clearly defined goal in mind before starting to search.

- STAY ON YOUR TRAIL: Don't explore every link or other interesting sites. Stay focused.

- STAY ORGANIZED: Have a plan for how you will store and use the information you find. Create folders to store downloaded files and make files into which you can cut and paste information.

- BUDGET YOUR TIME: Limit your searching on each topic to a predetermined amount of time.

- USE A FILTER: It's far easier than you think to accidentally stumble onto a pornographic Web site. Investigate the various filters available and use one!

SEARCH ENGINES THAT WILL SAVE YOU TIME

Your choice of a search engine makes a big difference in how effective you are with online research. Many search engines will yield a lot of unrelated results, but here are two that usually produce more pertinent search results:

Ask Jeeves

www.ask.com

This search engine allows you to write your search query as a simple question, such as, "Where is Timbuktu?" Ask Jeeves shows you the search results from several other search engines in addition to its own.

Google

www.google.com

Google ranks sites based on their popularity, so it's especially helpful if you're looking for information about something of interest to other people.

Ask Jeeves has answers for just about any question.

FINDING COLLEGE WEB SITES AND GUIDEBOOKS ONLINE

College Web sites are very handy for connecting with students and faculty, finding courses, and accessing specialized research. The typical site contains tuition and financial aid information, course catalogs, a calendar of events, contact information for faculty members, links to student Web pages, links to academic discussion groups, and sometimes even course syllabuses.

These Web sites can help you find colleges:

Yahoo Search

www.yahoo.com/Regional/Countries/United_States/Education/Colleges_and_Universities/

Use it for finding schools anywhere on the globe. Helpful indices contain e-mail addresses for colleges, college departments, and student clubs.

Embark

www.embark.com

This Web site will ask you a series of questions and then show you the Web sites of colleges that match your criteria. You'll even be able to apply online to the school of your choice.

Study Abroad

www.studyabroad.com

This site contains helpful links to college Web pages that describe distance-learning programs. This is a great resource if you are trying to do portfolio or independent study based on established programs.

EXCHANGING INFORMATION WITH STUDENTS AND FACULTY

The following list of sites is great for finding some of the latest information related to your studies. These sites can also help connect you to those individuals and organizations that are conducting the most up-to-date research in almost any field.

The World Lecture Hall

www.utexas.edu/world/lecture/

Contains links to pages created by faculty who use the Web to deliver course materials worldwide. Can easily be searched by course or subject. If you're looking for a syllabus to structure an independent study or a course description for a portfolio assessment, this site is the place to begin your search.

Scholarly Journals on the Web

info.lib.uh.edu/wj/webjour.html

A great place to find course descriptions and course syllabuses

This comprehensive directory provides links to numerous scholarly journals available on the Web. These journals are all free and require no registration or membership to receive them. Whatever you're studying, you'll find the most relevant information on all of the up-to-date research in the field.

Scholarly Societies on the Web
www.lib.uwaterloo.ca/society/webpages.html
Access over 1,400 online scholarly societies where professors and industry experts carry out discussions in their areas of expertise. You can use the site's search engine to locate societies that interest you.

Listservs
www.lsoft.com/lists/listref.html
Much like scholarly societies, listservs bring scholars together to share information on specific subjects. This site maintains a searchable, complete, up-to-date database of over 42,000 listservs!

GETTING THE STUDY MATERIALS YOU NEED
Previously, this was one of the most expensive elements of distance-learning education. However, you should not have to buy as many of your

required study materials since you can now access electronic versions online or get them through the library system. When looking for a difficult-to-find textbook, most students don't realize that although their local library may not have the needed book, another library within the system probably does. Your library's free interlibrary loan service provides you access to library collections worldwide! Plan ahead and put in a request to your library about a week before you need the study material. Most libraries let you borrow books for two to three weeks.

It can be challenging to renew interlibrary loan items, but it can be done. Usually, it will be as simple as standing by while your librarian calls the other library and renews the item over the phone. A small library will probably be more willing to do this. This way, you can keep materials for up to six weeks, more than enough time to complete your course if you use the accelerated learning methods in Part III. If you aren't going to use a book as a resource for continued reference, why buy it?

For the books that you do need to buy, I've listed a few sites for textbook exchanges and retailers offering student discounts.

First Search

newfirstsearch.oclc.org

This wonderful tool searches libraries around the world for the book you want. It is the easiest and most comprehensive way to search for library materials. You will have to use a login number and password to get into the site. Contact your local librarian and request the assigned login number and password for your specific library. The librarian should be happy to share them with you.

Here's how I used First Search:

1. I logged in and found the item I needed.

2. Using the e-mail feature, I sent myself an e-mail listing the item and libraries that had it.

3. I forwarded the e-mail to my librarian along with a message stating my request, library card number, and when I needed the item.

4. When the item arrived, usually some time during the following week, I was notified by phone or e-mail.

5. I drove three minutes to my library and picked up the materials I had requested!

Your library's free interlibrary loan service provides you access to library collections worldwide!

Berkeley Digital Library SunSite

sunsite.berkeley.edu

This site, maintained by Berkeley University, offers extensive electronic text and image collections.

Britannica Online

www.britannica.com

If you are looking for a quick fact or figure, this great resource probably has it. In addition to the entire Encyclopedia Britannica online, there are news stories, magazines, and books that are also available for browsing.

Interactive Learning Network

www.iln.net

Sign up for a free membership and gain access to online tutoring, subject lessons, video lectures, and handy subject reviews. Contains especially useful math- and science-related information.

Hungry Minds

www.hungryminds.com

This site has separate pages for each academic subject. Each subject page is maintained by a live "subject expert" and contains helpful information on

The Interactive Learning Network is a helpful site for test prep.

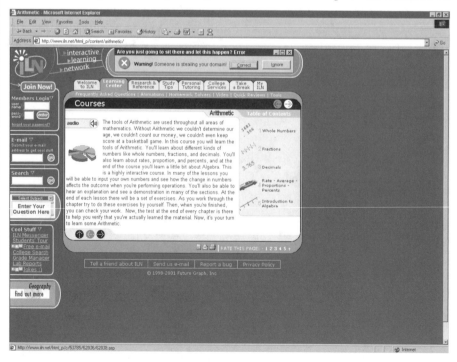

finding courses, book reviews, current research, answers to questions, and other resources on the Web, related to your course of study.

LOCATING STUDENT DISCOUNTS AND PURCHASING TEXTBOOKS

Student Advantage
www.studentadvantage.com

Numerous student discounts are available to registered, card-carrying members. Membership costs $20. This site is definitely worth checking out.

Campus Books
www.campusbooks.com

Use this search engine to price shop for new and used textbooks at fifteen member stores. Instead of visiting each store's site to compare prices on books, let Campus Books do the comparison shopping for you.

Textbooks at Cost
www.textbooksatcost.com

In addition to providing discounted textbooks, this site allows you to swap books directly with other students.

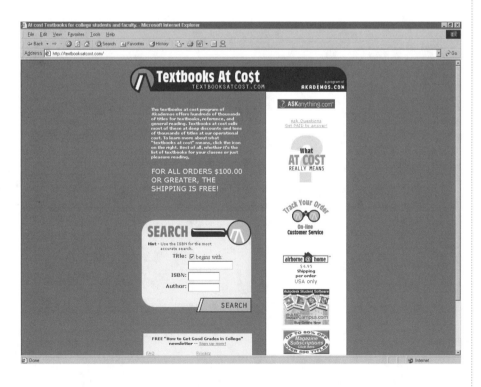

Find the textbook you need online and get a discount.

SIGNING UP WITH A SERVICE THAT WILL SAVE YOU MONEY

If you have multiple Internet users in your home, need a faster Internet connection, or are just tired of having your phone line always tied up when someone is online, consider ordering cable or Digital Subscriber Line, better known as DSL. While not available in all communities, these services continue to grow in popularity. If you are using such a high-speed internet service no additional telephone line is needed for connecting to the internet and allows for simultaneous access by multiple users. The cost usually ranges from $30 to $60 a month, which may be less than paying for a second phone line and monthly Internet access.

For more information on the availability and pricing of of high speed service in your area, call your local telephone company or check out their Web site.

Find out if DSL is the solution for your needs.

A CLEARING IN THE JUNGLE

I hope the jungle seems a little more manageable to you now. If you remember the pointers I've shared, your online research should be both rewarding and productive.

ACCELERATED LEARNING

You've been hiking for quite some time now, and you have a growing sense of accomplishment. Each dawn brings new trails to cover, new sights to see, and new challenges to anticipate. Then, looming in front of you, stands an incredibly massive, granite rock.

This is The Rock that causes all of the other trails to wind around, avoiding its precipitous slopes. Few will ever stand where you are, ready to tackle the challenge of climbing its heights, rather than taking the long and arduous trip around its perimeter.

You've seen very few hikers coming this way; the vast majority have chosen to take a trail which circles the rock on it's southern flank. While the other hikers won't have to struggle up the steep switchbacks, they will *lose many weeks in taking those cliff-skirting trails,* and *they will have to pay a hefty fee to the tour company that has sole access to the trails.*

Virtually a sheer cliff, The Rock has very few handholds on its face. At least that's what everyone thinks. The Guide Book tells a different tale: a tale of successful climbers, where they've sunk their pitons and bolts, and how they made it to the top with astonishing speed and safety. Although anxious about the climb, you aren't really worried that you won't make it. You have the rock-climbing equipment the Guide Book calls for.

You begin to climb, but your own weight seems like the enemy as you pull to lift yourself. Then, remembering the instructions in the Guide Book, you realize that you have to use your equipment correctly, or you won't make it. You begin to rely on your tools more than your strength, and you find that climbing becomes easier. Working with your tools and with the ropes, your hands become accustomed to anchoring the bolts. You realize now that you are climbing as a machine. Quickly, steadily, even easily, moving upwards. Using your climbing equipment becomes second nature, and you fly up the cliff.

Finally, your eyes crest the edge of the rock, and you can see sky all around you. You've made it to the top! Regaining your breath, you stand with arms stretched wide. Elation swells within you. You can see for miles in every direction. Of course, the direction which interests you most is west-ward, where Graduation Point lies. You can see it now for the first time.

As you turn back to collect your gear, you notice some small bright dots far below to the south. Gasping, you realize those are hikers, still miles from the bottom of the cliff! They have chosen the common route and are losing valuable time on the winding trails. You collect your gear, grateful for the tools you needed to take a direct route, right up a sheer cliff. You'll be using these friends again.

Whoever made the rule that learning had to be a long, time-consuming, difficult, and boring process? I'm here to tell you that no such rule exists. You were created with a natural capacity to explore, learn, and know. While most people choose to confine their learning to the classroom and subject themselves to processes that inhibit learning, you can begin taking charge of your education and enjoy the benefits of accelerated learning.

A whole new world of speed-reading, memory building, comprehension improvement, effective writing, and test-taking skills are awaiting your discovery. Not only will you find new ways to learn, but also new ways to apply your learning to your independent studies. Initially, utilizing these techniques will require a certain amount of determination and courage, but as you become familiar with them they will become second nature.

Soon, you will be learning at record speed, and through distance education, the rewards you receive will be incredible. Don't lose valuable time on Trail Normal. Accelerate your learning and head straight to Graduation Point!

The Power of Accelerated Learning:

An Introduction

9

B ecoming an accelerated learner is much easier and takes much less time than that which is required to learn most academic subjects. Because accelerated learning harmonizes with the way your brain naturally thinks and learns, acquiring these skills is an enjoyable and refreshing experience. I'm excited for you! By mastering these techniques, you'll be able to learn more than you ever dreamed possible. Plus, you'll learn it faster!

Principle #3: EFFICIENCY. Accelerated learning takes energy expended in the learning process, and makes you more productive.

FOUR STAGES OF ACCELERATED LEARNING:

Let's examine the four stages that you will pass through as you become an accelerated learner.

1. UNCONSCIOUS INCOMPETENCE. You simply don't know that you don't know. People at this stage are unaware of their brain's amazing potential to learn faster.

2. CONSCIOUS INCOMPETENCE. Knowing that you don't know. This is probably where you are right now in your learning journey. You are aware that accelerated learning exists, but you are still unsure of how to apply it to your studies.

3. CONSCIOUS COMPETENCE. Knowing that you know. Soon you will enter this stage as you begin using the accelerated learning

techniques. Getting to this stage will require concentration and diligence, similar to learning how to drive.

4. **Unconscious competence.** Not knowing that you know. After you've become experienced with accelerated learning techniques, you'll find that you begin to use them automatically. Suddenly, the way you approach your learning has been transformed. You now ARE an accelerated learner.

ARE YOU SEEKING EXCELLENCE OR A DEGREE?

Accelerated learning is a wonderful tool when used properly. More than just a fast way to get your degree, it's a way for you to develop a high level of skill and genuine understanding. If the only result of your independent studies is the acquisition of a degree, and you have not also achieved educational excellence, your degree has no real worth. You are a truly successful accelerated learner when you have improved not only the quantity and speed of your learning, but also the quality of your learning. How can this be accomplished?

1. By employing accelerated learning techniques that enable you to structure your learning in a way that works best for the brain

2. By moving learning from the classroom to the real world

3. By using the following Learning Gateway Questions

LEARNING GATEWAY QUESTIONS

One important step in making the transition from the classroom to independent study is learning how to ask effective questions. In a traditional classroom, the teacher asks a question and the students answer. With independent study, as you learn to formulate your own questions, not relying on others, you become your own teacher. Your study becomes a dialogue where you ask questions and search out the answers from your study materials. This study method has been around for thousands of years and has always been the most effective way to build true understanding.

There are some specific, key questions that apply to everything you'll learn. In the coming chapters, we'll look at how to use these key questions as part of the accelerated learning process. Here is a summary:

1. **What information is most important?** Your goal in studying anything is to identify the key information and then focus on learn-

> *"Everyone and everything around you is your teacher."*
> —Ken Keyes Jr.

> *"The important thing is not to stop questioning."*
> —Albert Einstein.

ing it well. You'll find an in-depth discussion of this question on page 101-103.

Perseverance is the key to any successful endeavor. "Never, never, never give up." —Winston Churchill

2. **What background information do I need in order to understand this?** Sometimes you can't completely master a subject until you have studied other foundational concepts. This question is addressed on page 103.

3. **What will the author's next point be?** Stay one step ahead of an author by trying to anticipate what they are going to say next. We'll look at this question more closely on page 103.

4. **Why am I studying this?** Before you begin studying something, define what you hope to get out of it. We'll examine this question in detail on page 104.

5. **How can I take "ownership" of this information?** You need to be able to restate what you've learned in your own words. This issue is dealt with on page 104.

6. **How does this information relate to what I already know?** Comparisons increase your understanding of new information, integrating it with what you have already learned. This question is explained on page 105.

7. **How will I remember this information?** Rather than relying on rote memorization, learn to use one of the memorization techniques explained in Chapter 11.

8. **What is the best way to organize vital information?** Learning maps and other techniques will keep you from being buried in words and will help you to outline the important points for easy memorization. I'll demonstrate how to do this on page 114-116.

9. **How do I apply what I have learned?** If you don't use it, you'll probably lose it! You'll find a discussion of this question on page 122.

Developing a questioning mind and becoming skilled in accelerated learning techniques will take time, but don't give up—anyone who consistently applies these techniques will become proficient.

Reading Power:

Breaking Through the 400 Barrier

"The end of reading is not more books, but more life."
—Holbrook Jackson

Do you think reading at high speeds while maintaining high comprehension is impossible? Howard Stephen Berg doesn't. According to the *Guinness Book of World Records*, he is the fastest reader in the world. Berg says he's no genius; he just applies the techniques you'll be learning in this chapter.

Just imagine how exciting it would be for you to double, triple, or even quadruple your reading speed. Wouldn't you like to start reading faster while comprehending even more? Wouldn't it be great if you could handle a much heavier course load and work at an accelerated pace? It *can* happen.

I used to think that I would never read more than 400 words per minute, but when I began learning accelerated reading techniques, my reading speed increased sharply. I gained a new skill, and my younger siblings gained a new form of entertainment—watching me flip through fat textbooks at a rate faster than a page per second. The librarian also took notice when I started visiting the library twice a week to keep up with my voracious reading. She would have been even more amazed if she had known that I regularly visit three other libraries! My brain is no bigger than yours. If I can do this, so can you!

In this chapter, we'll talk about how to transfer information from books to your brain quickly and effectively. In the next chapter, you'll learn how to use accelerated memory skills to boost your retention of information.

There are two challenges in mastering accelerated reading. One is to increase speed, the other is to increase comprehension. But first, you need to figure out why you read slowly.

WHAT'S SLOWING YOU DOWN?

1. **Reading aloud.** Sounding out every word forces you to spend time on unimportant words like "and," "but," and "the." Those words give structure to writing, but they are not nearly as important as the key nouns and verbs.

2. **Reading words individually.** Seeing words one at a time is much slower than seeing words in groups.

3. **Reading everything at the same speed.** Reading steadily from the beginning of the book to the end without changing pace means you're placing equal importance on all material.

4. **Stumbling over new words.** Pausing to consider the meaning of new vocabulary words slows you down.

HOW TO SPEED UP YOUR READING

1. STAY FOCUSED.

Eliminating distractions might be the single most important step in preparation for your reading. It is very important that you have a designated time and place for your study, free from the sounds of telephones, radios, and televisions.

Next, prepare yourself. Your mind should be alert but relaxed. Write down and forget your mental "to-do list" before you study. In addition, deal with any emotions of fear, worry, or anger. This includes any worries that you won't be able to learn the material.

2. CHANGE YOUR TECHNIQUE.

Most of us continue to read the way we were taught as children—one word at a time, one line at a time. This method mechanically slows your reading down to a pace that is much slower than your mind's capacity for receiving information. That's why reading is boring to many people.

The key is to read multiple words, lines, and even whole paragraphs simultaneously instead of one at a time. You can learn to see the words on the page and recognize their combined meaning without having to see and think about them individually. It is possible for your mind to become like a camera that views text quickly and in large sections. Few people can do this naturally; however, you can develop this skill by using hand motions to pace yourself and guide your eye.

If you're going to learn how to "view" the text, you must first practice some drills. Here are three of the most useful.

Guiding Finger Motion. Use your finger to guide your eye at a constant speed over each line of text, left to right. Choose a place to focus your eye, either just above your finger or in front of it, and keep your eye focused on following your finger. Don't stop or look at some other part of the text. This drill helps you stop back-skipping (looking back to see words you missed), a habit which slows you down.

Double Speed Drill. Using the guiding finger motion, move your eye over the text at twice the speed of your normal comprehension rate. The goal is to confuse the brain so that it no longer understands anything and thinks it must speed up. After doing this for several minutes, you should be able to slow down to a speed slightly faster than your normal comprehension rate, yet have normal comprehension.

Quadruple Speed Drill. Did you know that your brain is fully capable of reading multiple lines of text simultaneously? This is not just a technique for geniuses. To read at quadruple speed, use your finger to guide your eye across the text at twice your comprehension rate, but this time view two lines of text at a time. Again, don't worry about comprehension, just focus on viewing the text. Now you're moving along at four times your normal speed. After several minutes of this, slow down and start reading two lines of text at your normal reading speed. In time you should be able to simultaneously read two lines of text with normal comprehension.

If you practice these drills consistently for just fifteen minutes a day for one week, you will experience a remarkable change in how you read (you'll begin viewing text). You will also experience a dramatic increase in how fast you read.

3. Use multiple reading speeds.

I usually read a book through at least three times, but I do it faster and remember more than most people who read it just once. That's because I spend 10% of my time skimming, only 20% reading and studying, and an amazing 70% reviewing materials. I learned this "Master Level Reading" technique from Howard Stephen Berg. It is easy to learn and has helped me more than any other speed-reading technique. Here's how it works.

A. **Skimming.** Quickly skim over the entire book, noticing its design, various parts, special features, diagrams, and pic-

Tip: 20% of your efforts usually produce 80% of the value of your work.

tures. Jot down the key ideas being taught in each section and place a light pencil mark next to important parts you want to revisit. Skimming helps you identify and focus on the important while eliminating the trivial.

B. **Reading.** Read at your comprehension rate through the areas you determined are important. Remember, this rate will be much faster if you learn speed-reading techniques such as seeing the text in larger sections and skipping over meaningless words. As you read, mark especially important concepts that you want to study and memorize later.

C. **Studying.** The main focus of effective study involves extensive review and note taking. This is where you should spend most of your time if you're preparing for a test. Go back to the sections you previously identified as having special importance. Study these sections further, increasing your ability to recall by using the memorization methods explained in the next chapter.

D. **Reviewing.** Quickly go back over the book, allowing the information presented in the text to trigger your memory of the key information you studied. Multiple reviews make multiple impressions in your memory and assist in long-term retention of information.

Most students approach their reading with the assumption that all the information presented has equal value. Therefore, they read every word and every page with the same speed, intensity, and interest. This only results in slow progress, confusion, and eventual discouragement (after the exam). Don't waste your time doing this!

You must identify important information to focus on, less important information to skim over, and trivial information to skip altogether. Most books are 80% minor ideas and facts and 20% major ideas and facts. Aim to spend 20% of your time skimming the 80% of minor details and 80% studying the 20% of important material. When I applied this principle to my college studies, my study speed immediately tripled. When I worked on the courses in my specialization, my study speed was even faster. Frequently, the courses' content would overlap, so I could just skim the material, find the new information I needed, and simply focus on that.

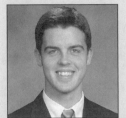

STUDENT'S POINT OF VIEW: *Speed-Reading—A Good Idea Even for Non Speed-Readers*
Name: *Kyle Yates*
Home State: *Florida*
Major: *Bachelor of Science in Business Administration*
College: *Thomas Edison*
Age at graduation: *Currently enrolled*
Current age: *19*

I'm just starting to learn speed-reading skills, but already they have helped me to accelerate my learning. Before I took Howard Berg's speed reading course, I was an inefficient reader and didn't think that speed-reading would work for me. Now that I have practiced speed-reading drills and understand how to apply the new techniques to my college studies, I realize that it is possible for anyone to increase their reading speed. My speed, comprehension rate, focus, and memory have all improved. Although I'm only doing part-time study, these new skills have enabled me to complete an average of three credits per week toward my degree. The skills I have learned are essential for success in my distance learning, but more importantly, they will continue to benefit me throughout life.

Often, a textbook explains an important concept in a paragraph or two and then gives pages and pages of examples and case studies. Study the concept and skim over the rest.

When I was studying for the CLEP test on Information Systems and Computer Applications, I already knew about computer hardware and software from using a computer. But I had never learned computer programming and some of the technical terminology. So, when I prepared for the test, I skimmed my books to find and study just the information that taught basic programming and new terminology.

Perhaps you think speed-reading won't work for you because you read books that are very technical or are 100% important information. This is a total misconception. The Master Level Reading method is proven effective for even technical subjects.

Probably the most difficult subject for me is math. But I have learned that speed-reading even math books is very helpful.

First, I skim the book quickly. At this stage I don't comprehend any of the formulas or what I'm reading. But, I do gain some very critical information about how the book is structured. I also identify both the number and type

FROM THE EXPERT: *Accelerated Learning—The Key to Distance Learning Success*

NAME: *Howard Stephen Berg*
POSITION: *President of Mega Learning Corporation and the world's fastest reader.*

Why is it that when you read a book for work or school, you can't even remember the title or author's name just fifteen minutes after putting it down? Yet you can remember silly songs, word for word, without even trying. Why does this happen? When I first asked myself this question, I had no idea it would lead me to become the world's fastest reader. I simply wanted to know why the brain retains so much useless information and often deletes more important data. The solution to this problem drove me to discover a more effective way to read, comprehend, and retain information.

Your brain is designed to retain information that frequently repeats, is emotionally intense, is associated with a specific rhythm, or has powerful contextual clues. When listening to a song played on the radio, the music's rhythm automatically helps install it into your permanent memory.

Understanding how these four brain stimulants can ignite your memory is the first step towards becoming a better learner—an essential skill for surviving in today's world. It's been said that every ninety days the world's information content doubles. It's also been said that more information has been generated in the past century than all previous history combined. Without strategies for reading faster, improving comprehension, and retaining information, how do you expect to avoid making costly mistakes from poor decisions based on inadequate knowledge?

Distance learning is one solution to this problem. Offering you the opportunity to download new information directly to your computer at a convenient learning time frees you from having to learn at a specific time and place that might not fit into your schedule. I believe that linking accelerated learning tools to the information provided by distance-learning providers will fuse the learning benefits of accelerated learning with the convenience of distance learning. We are on the threshold of a new learning revolution as great as the invention of the printing press. For the first time, anyone can instantly access t he information they need to succeed in today's information-rich world. Linked to accelerated learning, they will also be able to store and retrieve it when needed.

For those prepared to take full advantage of this learning revolution will come opportunities for success unheard of by those who have lived in the past. Invest a little time in a good learning program like Maximum Speed Reading and plunge into a new world of distance-learning opportunities with the skills and confidence you need for success in today's fast-paced world.

of formulas presented, as well as the relationships of formulas and major mathematical concepts.

Later, when I actually read the book, I often condense key formulas and concepts into a single page of material to be memorized. Yes, 100% of the book is important, but often 80% of the information is nothing more than a further explanation of the vital points. Once I understood the 20% of key formulas and concepts, I didn't need to spend time on the 80% of additional explanations.

INCREASING YOUR COMPREHENSION AND RETENTION

Accelerated reading is more than simple speed-reading. It also includes attaining maximum comprehension and retention levels. Let's examine six of the most useful ways to increase comprehension and retention.

1. **UNDERSTAND THE FORMAT.**

One of the easiest, most effective ways to boost your reading comprehension is to approach each reading assignment with a clear understanding of how the book is formatted and how to use it most productively.

The front and rear jackets. Don't skip these! These key texts usually explain why the book was written and why reading it will benefit you. Knowing this information up front will help you form your "expert questions." It tells you what you should be looking for.

The foreword, preface, and introduction. From these you can learn what factors influenced the author to write the book.

The introduction often tells how the book is laid out and in what order the chapters should be read. Sometimes, it will even contain a paragraph of information that summarizes the most important points in each section or chapter. This is *key information!*

A book's foreword may be written by someone other than the author and will help you see the subject from another perspective. Classic books often have a new foreword explaining the book's influence or importance in light of current events.

The table of contents. Examining the table of contents at least twice before reading the rest of the book will provide the big picture of how the book is organized. Later the table of contents and your own notes can be used to make a learning map.

Question 1: What information is most important?

Question 2: What background information do I need in order to understand this?

Question 3: 'What will the author's next point be?

Principle #2: THOROUGHNESS. You must examine the accuracy of everything you learn.

Charts, tables, and diagrams. These helpful tools will allow you to visualize the data being presented in the text. Spend extra time reviewing the important ones. Remember, a picture is truly worth a thousand words!

The glossary. This is probably my favorite part of any book. I read this part first to get an idea of the book's difficulty. When I see a word I don't know, I associate it with a mental picture so that when I encounter it again in the text, I can easily remember what it means.

2.   READ WITH A PURPOSE.

Before opening the book, know why you are reading it and what you need to learn from it. If you are preparing for an exam, determine whether that exam requires a general or an in-depth knowledge of the subject. On what areas will it focus? Having these answers from the start will ensure that you don't waste time studying irrelevant information.

3.   READ ACTIVELY RATHER THAN PASSIVELY.

Question 4: Why am I studying this?

It's dangerous to just read and blindly accept information. To gain true understanding you must "talk" with the writer and "question" him, as if you were discussing the book face to face. In the back of your mind, keep asking, "Why are you saying this? What do you really mean? Why did you leave important information out?" After asking these questions, go back and restate the writer's main points in your own words. Explain why you agree or disagree or tell some additional facts you know about the subject.

A questioning mind will always be your most useful learning tool.

4.   RETHINKING, SUMMARIZING, VISUALIZING; NOTING THE IMPORTANT POINTS; LEARNING MAPS

As you read a book, create a mental outline of its contents. Set aside some time after completing each section to cement your thoughts on the subject and make sure that what you've read makes sense to you. Distinguish between the important and unimportant information. Chapter divisions provide a natural stopping point for doing this.

Question 5: How can I take "ownership" of this information?

Once you have created a mental outline and identified the concepts that are important to you, use accelerated memory techniques to lock in this key data. One technique that you can use for remembering key points is the "learning map." We'll be learning more about this and other exciting accelerated learning techniques in Chapter 11.

5.   **INTEGRATE NEW KNOWLEDGE WITH EXISTING KNOWLEDGE.**

It's difficult to master large volumes of information in a short amount of time. To make sense of it all, you must compare this new information with things you already know. How are they different? How are they similar?

If you're learning about the supply and demand curves for major commodities, think about how supply and demand have affected the prices in your grocery store. If you are learning about the British system of government, compare it to the U.S. system of government.

This kind of thought process is referred to as thinking in analogies. Analogies accelerate the speed at which you learn by helping you to connect your short-term memory with your long-term memory.

6.   **SCHEDULE YOUR READING.**

Have you ever read a chapter and then discovered that you could hardly recall anything that you just read? If you think back, what parts of the chapter do you remember most? Studies show that if you're like most people, you probably remember information from the beginning and the end of the reading session. Thus, in order to increase your recall, increase the number of starts and stops in your studying! In other words, instead of studying for a solid hour, try breaking your study period into three, twenty-minute sections divided by five-minute breaks. Frequent breaks will give your brain time to process the information you've just read.

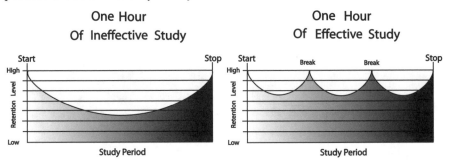

Also, determine when you are able to achieve maximum concentration and schedule your study periods during that time. Don't let this time get crowded out by other tasks!

Analogies accelerate the speed at which you learn by helping you to connect your short-term memory with your long-term memory.

Question 6: How does this information relate to what I already know?

MAXIMUM SPEED READING

To master these concepts, I recommend that you get your own copy of the *Maximum Speed Reading* program. Unlike other speed-reading programs, it's easy to understand, easy to apply, and not time-consuming. Most importantly, it works! Speed-reading is not just for "school"; it's a skill you'll be able to use for the rest of your life. There are few investments you will make in life that will ever pay such rich dividends. For details see our *Student Success Catalog*.

Memory Power:

Unlocking Your Brain

11

Y ou don't want to forget it. It's important to you. What do you do? You tell yourself, "Remember, remember, remember!" However, simple repetition is not an effective way to learn! How do most of us recall what we have learned and memorized? "Think, think, think," we tell the brain, hoping this will bring back the information. Unfortunately, these methods are unreliable and a foolish waste of your brain's amazing potential.

The reason that accelerated learning strategies are so powerful is because they work in harmony with your brain's natural design.

YOUR BRAIN: A VAST RESOURCE OF UNUSED POTENTIAL

Scientists who study the brain have discovered that most people never use more than 10 percent of their brain's capacity. Perhaps you have heard this statistic before, but have you ever wondered why it is true? The reason most people never tap into 90 percent of their brain's potential is that when we memorize, we fail to organize information in a way that makes sense to the brain. The latest research shows that the brain:

1. Utilizes multisensory pathways for learning,

2. Stores information as pictures,

3. Thinks in chains,

4. Employs long-term and short-term memory, and

5. Sorts information.

The purpose of this chapter is to show you how to structure your learning around these facts. Soon, you will be able to begin tapping into the amazing capacity of your brain.

"Your brain is like a sleeping giant."
—Tony Buzan

USING MULTISENSORY PATHWAYS FOR LEARNING

There are three basic pathways for learning:

VISUAL. Visual learning is best accomplished by viewing pictures, diagrams, demonstrations, and videos. A visual learner will tend to mentally visualize what he's studying.

AUDITORY. This learning is characterized by listening to discussions, debates, lectures, and verbal instructions. An auditory learner is most effective when he reads aloud or gives oral summaries of what he has studied.

KINESTHETIC. Kinesthetic learning is typified by moving, touching, and experiencing. A kinesthetic learner benefits from hands-on learning, writing things down, learning in groups, and moving around while he studies.

Although we all learn through each of these three pathways, almost everyone has a tendency to learn best through just one of them. Take the time to discover what type of learner you are and then develop a learning strategy that emphasizes the pathway through which you learn best. For example, I'm a visual learner. I visualize concepts as I read about them, draw pictures for the main points (visual); ask and answer questions aloud about what I am reading (auditory); and write out a list of the major points (kinesthetic). Notice how I emphasize the visual pathway.

STORING INFORMATION AS PICTURES

Your mind operates like a sophisticated video camera. Everything you see is recorded as detailed pictures. For example, I know you've looked at the cover of this book many times. Look at it now, then close your eyes and recall as many things about the cover as you can. Could you recall the orange, brown, and blue colors used on the cover, the large modern looking fonts, the globe and the book, and where they were positioned? You probably remembered all this information and more. On the other hand, if I should verbally describe the cover of this book to you, could you recall the details? *Probably not!* Why the difference? Compared to words, pictures can store much greater amounts of information. **If you want to store volumes of information quickly, learn to store it visually.** More than a cliché, truly "a picture is worth a thousand words."

Let's look at some strategies for how you can store information as pictures. But some of you are saying, "Wait a minute! I'm not a visual learner!" That's fine, but the following two facts are still true:

1. Pictures store vast amounts of information.
2. Everyone is able to learn through the visual pathway.

Later we'll discuss how to adapt these visual learning strategies for auditory and kinesthetic learners.

THINKING IN CHAINS

Our brains can serve as a file cabinet, sorting information and storing it by subject. Unfortunately, most people don't tap into this ability, and their brains resemble a file cabinet that's been dumped out all over the floor. When they want to remember something, they throw it on top of the pile in their brain, hoping to find it later.

Our brains work best with long chains of information. Information stored in a long series of connected bits is easier to remember than information stored as single bits of unconnected, unrelated information. To the brain, "unconnected" and "unrelated" means unimportant, uninteresting, and unusable. Here are several simple ways to sort and store information in chains.

Association List

The Association List creates a mental link between two things. A visual learner might use an association list like this to remember numbers.

0.	Cheerios	Round with a hole in the middle
1.	Skyscraper	Tall and thin
2.	Shoes	One for each foot
3.	Triangle	Three sides
4.	Car	Four doors, four wheels
5.	Hand	Five fingers
6.	Muffin tin	Six muffin cups
7.	Gas station	7-11 Gas station
8.	Stick of butter	Eight tablespoons in one stick
9.	Baseball team	Nine players

An auditory learner might make up a rhyming list, e.g., One–Gun, Two–Shoe, Three–Tree. A kinesthetic learner might make up a rhyming list of actions, e.g., One–Run, Two–Do pushups, Three–Climb a tree.

It's much easier to recall a series of numbers when images, sounds, or actions are associated with them.

"Your brain operates like a file cabinet. The more you place memos, letters, reports, notes, and documents into their proper files— the more organized you are—the easier it is to retrieve things when you need them."
—Kevin Trudeau

Now, let's say you want to remember the year Lincoln delivered his address at Gettysburg, 1863. Start by visualizing the pictures that represent each number in order—1, Skyscraper; 8, Butter; 6, Muffin Tin; and 3, Triangle.

Stories of the Mind

After building your mental list of pictures, link them together in a story. For our example, we would include both the historical event (the Gettysburg Address) and the number pictures in our story. Imagine Abraham Lincoln reciting the Gettysburg Address (event) while standing on a skyscraper (1) that falls on a stick of butter (8). The stick of butter splatters onto six muffins (6) sitting on a triangular plate (3). Notice the use of vivid actions to link the pictures together in this story.

If you are able to strongly link your number pictures to the picture of Lincoln giving the Gettysburg address, remembering the year will be no problem. Imagine Lincoln speaking, and you'll remember your number pictures. Does this sound like a lot of work just to remember one date in history? It might take you a long time to recite this list of pictures and actions, but with practice you'll be able to see it in your mind's eye faster than I can say "1863." Practice using the number association list, and you will speed up your recall of the pictures that represent each number.

Another way to create strong links is to include music (if you're an auditory learner) or through personally interacting with the pictures (if you're a kinesthetic learner). For example, instead of seeing Lincoln standing on the skyscraper, the auditory learner might imagine hearing Lincoln say something about the tower as part of his speech, or think of a musical piece that seems to describe what's happening, or imagine hearing loud sound effects as the tower begins falling over. The kinesthetic learner will interact with the pictures by picking Lincoln up, placing him on the tower, kicking it over, and then cleaning up all the butter that missed the muffins on the triangular plate.

This strategy can be adapted for memorizing complicated mathematical formulas, scientific equations, the table of elements, tables of financial data, or any other numbers.

The Name Game

Auditory learners can best associate things through sounds and music. For example, suppose you are taking German and need to learn a word list. You can remember this list of words by thinking of English words that sound similar and visualizing them in a way that links them with the corresponding German word. The table below gives examples.

English Word	German Word	Similar-Sound Picture
Soup	Suppen	**Soup** bowl with a **pen** floating in it.
Meat	Fleisch	A large piece of **flesh** that will be cooked for meat.
Eggs	Eier	A dozen eggs floating in the **air**.
Fruit	Obst	An **obst**inate orange that can't be peeled.
Cheese	Kase	A large **case** of cheese.

The Acronym

An acronym compresses a large amount of information into a quick sequence of letters. For example, we all know the meaning of FBI and CIA. The fictitious character ROY G. BIV helps us remember the colors of the rainbow—red, orange, yellow, green, blue, indigo, and violet.

You can also use the first letters of a series of words to make a more memorable series of words that start with the same letters. For example, you could easily remember each of the memorization techniques (ASNAC) explained in this section like this:

Association List	Active
Story	Stories
Name Game	Nicely
Acronym	Assist
Chunking	Creative memorization

Chunking

Were you ever required to memorize a poem, speech, or long story? We usually remember the first and last parts, but it's easy to forget the middle. You can eliminate this problem by dividing the passage into chunks and picking a key word or phrase to identify each chunk. You could use the first letter of all your chunks to make an acronym for additional ease in memorization.

The ideas above are simple suggestions that I hope will help you begin creating your own mnemonics and pictures. These techniques have thousands of applications awaiting your discovery.

"The chief aid to memory is order."
—Simonides

Question 7: How will I remember this information?

CONNECTING SHORT-TERM MEMORY TO LONG-TERM MEMORY

We have difficulty recalling information because our memory is divided between long-term memory and short-term memory. Although our brain records all of the experiences and instruction we receive, most of this information is recorded only in short-term memory. We must transfer the information we want to remember from short-term memory into long-term memory. Probably the most effective way to do this is by pegging.

Here are the basic steps of **pegging**:

1. CREATE A PEG LIST. Identify twenty items that you interact with every day, such as the rooms in your house, parts of your body, or parts of your car. Divide the list into four distinct groups with five items each. These are your twenty pegs.

2. SEE THE PEG LIST IN YOUR MIND. Visualize each of the pegs in your mind. You should be able to see each peg with clarity, color, and detail. Go through the list in your mind seeing each peg one by one. Then try to see all five pegs within a section at one time. Finally, see all the pegs in your list at once. Your goal is to be able to instantly flash the picture of your entire peg list before your mind's eye.

3. ATTACH YOUR INFORMATION TO THE PEGS. Now that your peg list is held in your long-term memory, you're ready to store new information on it. Individually attach the items you want to remember to the pegs on your peg list using action, stories, movement, color, or anything else that helps you associate the item with the peg. The important thing here is that you create the connection, because what you create, you remember. The connections you create don't have to make sense to anyone but you.

4. REVIEW THE PEGS. Visualize each peg with the information you attached to it. Then, do whole groups at once. Finally, visualize the entire peg list with all attached items. Do this until you can see all of the items within a fraction of a second.

We must transfer the information we want to remember from short-term memory into long-term memory.

The sample house list (next page) demonstrates the correct arrangement of *pegs*—four groupings of five pegs for a total of twenty pegs. Once the pegs are firmly established in your memory, your house list is ready for information to be attached to the pegs through creative association.

My House List

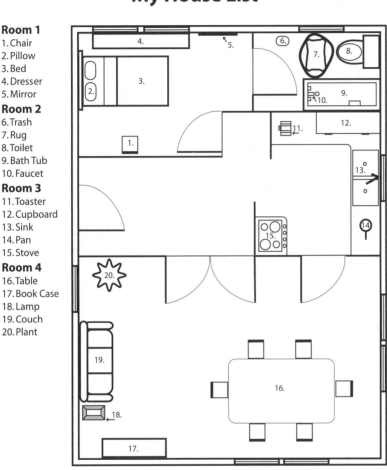

Room 1
1. Chair
2. Pillow
3. Bed
4. Dresser
5. Mirror

Room 2
6. Trash
7. Rug
8. Toilet
9. Bath Tub
10. Faucet

Room 3
11. Toaster
12. Cupboard
13. Sink
14. Pan
15. Stove

Room 4
16. Table
17. Book Case
18. Lamp
19. Couch
20. Plant

I found that by going through this process I could instantly recall long lists of complicated information simply by seeing my entire peg list in my mind's eye. This was a tremendous help when I took tests!

Once you establish your initial peg list, you can expand the number of pegs you have by making new lists. Anything you interact with daily that has many distinct parts will work for a peg list. I found that a list of sixty pegs allowed me to move at a fast pace. But what if you use up all of your pegs? No problem—reuse them. You don't need to worry about getting the lists mixed up. If you use your house list to peg twenty new math formulas and later that

Once you establish your initial peg list, you can expand the number of pegs you have by making new lists.

day use the same list to peg twenty new biology terms, you won't get them confused. I sometimes used the same pegs four times in one day, and my lists didn't get mixed up.

Pegging enables me to recall all of the information that I stored as well as recall the information in order. If I had pegged a list of thirty items, and you came along and asked me, "What's item number 17?" I would be able to tell you immediately. Pegging can be used to remember lists of historical events, step-by-step formulas and plans, key points of an essay, and long lists of important terminology.

SORTING AND STORING INFORMATION

We've already seen how representing information visually makes it easier to remember. "Learning maps" take this idea a step further.

Linear presentation of information in sequential outlines uses only a tiny fraction of your brain's capacities. Learning maps are a "whole brain" approach to learning. They simultaneously stimulate left-brain functions (words, numbers, lists, sequences, and analyses) and right-brain functions (color, imagery, dimension, and spatial awareness).

Your brain connects information more like the branches of a tree than a series of arrows. Linear note taking is like a series of arrows, but a learning map is like a "tree." Learning maps harmonize with your brain's design, and that's why they're so effective.

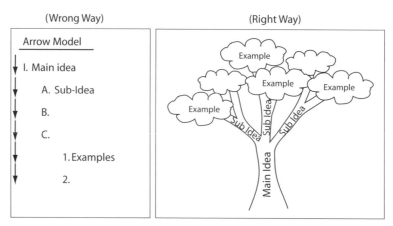

Principle # 7: UNDERSTANDING. The goal of education is to reach a higher level of understanding.

To construct a learning map, place your main subject at the center with secondary information branching out from it. Add further details and examples on the corresponding branches.

Learning Map

An example of a learning map, based on the content of this chapter.

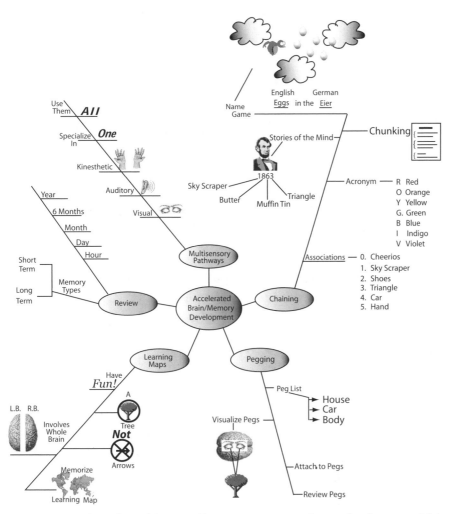

Representing ideas this way allows you to not only see the themes within a subject, but also visualize the relationship between themes.

Pictured above is an example of a learning map, based on the content of this chapter.

Notice how the learning map allows you to visualize, have fun with, and animate your information. The most memorable and effective learning maps use the following multisensory features:

Question 8: What is the best way to organize vital information?

- **Pictographs:** Little sketches present large amounts of information quickly and memorably.

- **Color:** The more color your learning map contains, the easier it'll be to remember.

- **Action:** Animate the subject! Add illustrations and lines that indicate movement.

- **Humor:** Things that are fun and make us laugh are easier to learn.

- **Creative Links:** Your symbols for links can also have significance. You can give different meanings to different links, such as large arrows, small arrows, long squiggles, or short lightning bolts.

- **Clear Lettering:** Print words, place them directly on the line, and write only one word per line.

- **Key Words:** Don't write complete sentences, just key words and important terms you want to remember.

- **Numbered Lists:** The wonderful thing about numbered lists is that you can attach them to a peg list for instant recall.

I find that creating a learning map is much more enjoyable than writing normal linear notes. Don't get carried away with all the fun though. Make sure that your learning maps are easy to understand; if they aren't, you'll encounter trouble when you come back for review. Clarity of information is more important than quantity of information.

After creating a learning map, recalling it becomes the simple and enjoyable task of viewing the learning map once again in your mind. If you create a learning map for an entire course of study, you'll be able to recall it almost instantly by glancing at it in your mind's eye. Develop maps for an entire year's worth of study, and within a few minutes you can review all the courses you've taken, recalling even very detailed information about each one!

MEMORIZING YOUR LEARNING MAPS

1. DRAW THE MAP ON PAPER. Make sure that it is full of action and humor. Use symbols and pictures to emphasize key concepts. Show strong connections between relationships of items on the map.

2. RECREATE THE MAP IN YOUR MIND'S EYE. After looking at your complete map on paper, close your eyes and visualize it in your mind's eye.

3. DUPLICATE THE ORIGINAL LEARNING MAP WITHOUT LOOKING AT IT. As you draw it, try to remember how it looks in your mind.

4. COMPARE THE TWO LEARNING MAPS. Compare the original learning map and the one you made from memory. Your mind will instantly focus on what's missing in your recreated map. This process reinforces and trains the memory.

5. DRAW THE FINAL LEARNING MAP. Now that you know what areas you missed, redraw the entire learning map from memory with all the details.

6. PRACTICE FLASHING THIS MAP in your mind until you can visualize the entire map instantly.

To learn more about this and other effective note-taking strategies, check out the *Student Success Catalog* for information about the new *Mega Note Taking* course by Andrew Pudewa.

DAILY LEARNING CYCLE

While you sleep, your brain sorts out the information it has received during the day and consolidates it into long-term memory. You can use this understanding of sleep to your benefit by reviewing the things you have learned before going to bed. Here's the procedure:

1. Learn new material.
2. Review what you've learned.
3. Sleep.
4. Review previous day's learning soon after you wake up.

LONG-TERM LEARNING CYCLE

By using these memorization strategies, you can have excellent recall of very detailed information. However, even long-term memory can dull over time. To keep the "rust" off the facts in your long-term memory, use this proven strategy:

1. Learn new material.
2. Within one hour review what was learned.
3. The next day review again.
4. After one month review again.
5. After six months review again.
6. After one year review again.

While you sleep, your brain sorts out the information it has received during the day and consolidates it into long-term memory.

To alert you when to review what, enter a reminder on your calendar or in your computer. If you store your learning maps in a file, you can access and review an entire course within minutes.

This discipline will pay off! If you follow this cycle, you will permanently lock the information you have learned into your long-term memory.

LEARNING THROUGH MUSIC

Virtually every student recognizes $e=mc^2$ as Einstein's theory of relativity, but very few people realize that the key to unlocking Einstein's creative genius was music. An accomplished violinist, Einstein was a connoisseur of fine music. Classical music, especially music by Mozart and Haydn, was a powerful force that activated the creative part of his brain and enabled him to come up with amazing scientific breakthroughs. When Einstein was working, if he got to a point where his thought processes hit a wall, he would pick up a violin and play it. By activating this creative, artistic side of his brain, he was able to go back to work and think "out of the box" once again.

The most recent research on the brain concludes that music has a dramatic effect on human learning processes. Listening to classical and baroque music works in harmony with these processes and puts the mind into an ideal state for maximum learning. This has been referred to as "relaxed alertness." On the other hand, listening to rock music confuses these processes and has a destructive effect on the brain. It has been demonstrated that rock music will often trigger an entire series of mental, physical, and emotional disturbances.

I have found that pacing my reading with baroque music enables me to study longer, remember better, and ultimately get better grades. Sometimes, I must contend with the noise of people talking in the background, my brothers playing in the next room, or the telephone ringing. However, turning on some baroque music enables me to "tune out" the distractions and concentrate on my studies.

Researchers in Bulgaria have developed this form of music-based learning even further. Using slow, 60-beat baroque music, they have been able to teach students to converse fluently in a foreign language in only thirty days!

Among the benefits to be gained from listening to baroque music are improved listening skills, greater concentration, and vocabulary development. In addition, if you are a musician yourself, playing a musical instru-

The most recent research on the brain concludes that music has a dramatic effect on human learning processes.

ment actually reshapes your brain by stimulating the formation of additional neural networks.

For more information on accelerated learning through music, go to musica.ps.uci.edu.

MY PERSONAL SUCCESS WITH ACCELERATED MEMORY

Before I understood memorization techniques, I couldn't even remember a list of five items I needed from the grocery store. I'd read a book and forget what I read as soon as I finished it. I'd hear a new word in a foreign language class and immediately forget it. But those days are long gone!

In 1998, I taught English in China for six months. I had a very busy teaching schedule but made significant progress learning Chinese using the above techniques. For instance, I tried to learn through each multisensory pathway.

VISUAL. I used pegging to visualize new words and remember them in orderly lists.

AUDITORY. I regularly listened to Chinese audiotapes and took every opportunity to engage in conversation. I also listened to baroque music while studying.

KINESTHETIC. During exercise times each day, I recited lists of memorized Chinese words and practiced talking about the actions I was doing.

After only six months, I had reached a proficiency in Chinese equal to two years of intensive study in a traditional college!

This remarkable progress was not because I have an unusual talent for language acquisition. My friend Simeon was overwhelmed by the idea of learning Chinese because he lacked natural linguistic ability. Before he left for China, he asked me to explain the memory techniques I'd used. Simeon adapted them to his own learning style and became fluent in only five months! You will be amazed at how these techniques will help you too!

DYNAMIC MEMORY

I trust this chapter has challenged and inspired you to begin using your brain's full potential. In order to truly master these concepts, I recommend that you obtain the accelerated learning course I have developed called *Dynamic Memory and Study Skills*. See the Student Success Catalog at the end of this book for details.

Writing Power:

Structure, Style, and Speed

Does the idea of writing college papers give you the jitters? Take heart. When I wrote my first college paper, I was apprehensive too—but after learning the following techniques, I never earned less than an "A" on my papers!

Since distance-learning courses often rely heavily on writing assignments, it is imperative that you learn to write well and fast!

THE WRITE RIGHT AWAY WRITING TECHNIQUE

When should you start the process of writing your paper? The answer may surprise you, but it is very important: Begin the writing process before you even read your study material! Most students put off writing until just before the deadline, but the secret to accelerated writing is developing your plan for the writing project as soon as you start the course. Here's a simple three-step approach:

1. Find out the format required for your writing project.

2. Outline your subject with learning maps as you study the subject.

3. Do the writing.

1. Find out the required format for your writing project and decide what type of outline to use.

Make sure you know exactly what kind of papers you are expected to write before you delve into that stack of reading material. Usually, you'll receive a course syllabus that clearly outlines what writing projects will be assigned. Also, give special attention to any additional instructions that are provided by your professor. Before you start writing, find out the answers to these questions:

TIP: *Have the end in view before you even begin.*

What is the required format? You cannot use the same essay format for every writing assignment. You may be required to respond to a series of questions, present your paper in outline form, or write a full-fledged persuasive essay.

What depth is required? Some assignments ask you to present a broad or general overview of a subject; others require you to write in detail about a specific aspect of the subject.

Is there a required layout? Font, margins, line spacing, footnote appearance, paper orientation, and how your personal identification information is arranged—these details matter considerably to your professor. If a specific layout is not requested, become familiar with writing standards by referring to *The Greggs Reference Manual.*

How many pages or words are required? Try to stay within these guidelines and never assume that your professor will appreciate your "initiative" in writing more pages than required. Quality is much more important than quantity.

What style and how much documentation is required? The most common formats for documenting research are the American Psychological Association style (APA) and the Modern Language Association style (MLA).

TIP: *Write what the professor likes.*

What kind of writing does my professor prefer to see? You must adjust your writing style to the tastes of your professor. Some delight to see oodles of creativity with vivid adjectives and active verbs, while others are merely concerned with the basic presentation of objective facts. After I turned in one very polished essay, my professor wrote in bold, red letters, "This is not a creative writing course, just the facts, please."

Professors who teach in large schools will usually have very little time to review your papers. However, those who teach distance-learning courses will often pay more attention to your papers and provide more feedback. All of my professors took time to write comments and suggestions on my papers. Not only did these notes aid my learning, but they showed me how to write more effectively for that professor in the future.

Can I use the writing assignment to focus on a topic that will be helpful to me in other areas of life? Often, with distance learning, there is more freedom to focus your assignments on areas that interest you. If a certain aspect of the subject you are studying might be important to your future work, try to focus your writing on that aspect. One assignment in a business communication course required me to select an example of international bargaining that

Question 9: How do I apply what I have learned?

resulted in a communication breakdown, then write a paper identifying the reasons for the breakdown. I focused on U.S.-China relations—a topic that greatly interests me. After completing this enjoyable assignment, I received an A and many positive comments from the instructor. Remember, Accelerated Distance Learning is about learning for life.

How many topics am I to write about, and what will they be? You probably won't be able to choose your thesis until step three, Do the Writing. But, begin thinking about what your topics will be before you even start reading your textbook. Go ahead and choose your topics based on whatever you know about the subject. (If you really know nothing about the subject, skim your reading assignment and try to spot potential candidates for topics.) As you read the textbook, continue evaluating your choices, narrowing the scope of them if possible. By pre-selecting topics, you will be able to focus your studies around your anticipated writing assignment.

What type of writing outline will I use? After skimming the material, modify the following basic descriptive essay model to fit your subject.

Descriptive Essay Model

I. Introduction
   1. } Get attention of the reader.
   2. } Provide Background Information (time, place, context).
   3. }
   4. } State three topics.
   5. }

II. }
III. } BODY PARAGRAPHS — same as topic report model
IV. }

V. Conclusion
   1. }
   2. } Restate three topics.
   3. }
   4. State the *most significant* thing and why; comment; analyze.
   5. What is the meaning or importance of this information? Never use "I."

If you were asked to write a descriptive essay on distance learning, you would choose three topics (e.g., academics, cost, and social opportunity) and then write two paragraphs per topic, explaining and describing each one. For a longer essay, it would be a simple matter to add more topics, subtopics, or paragraphs per topic.

TIP: Write what will help you prepare for your future.

This essay model is also adaptable for other types of essays. A persuasive essay is divided between providing arguments for and dispelling arguments against a given proposition. A "compare and contrast" essay presents two issues next to each other for orderly comparison. An historical essay is usually arranged chronologically. In each of these essay types, the basic structure remains the same.

2.   Outline your subject with learning maps as you study the subject.

By developing the notes you need for your writing project as you study, you will save time: you won't need to reread the same material after you begin writing, and you will be able to stay focused on the information that is important to your writing assignment.

After choosing a specific writing outline for your paper in step one, you will need a method for outlining your reading and research as you begin to study. Now it's time to use the learning map explained in Chapter 11. Make keyword notes of the important facts and visualize the complex relationships between various topics within the subject. You can make a map for a whole subject, a topic, or even a subtopic. Later, when you're writing and need to refresh your memory on an important concept, just review your learning map.

The wonderful thing about the learning map method is that it requires that you discover connections between ideas. You need to be able to demonstrate to your professors how the whole picture fits together. The more easily you can visualize the relationships between the concepts, the more easily you will be able to write in a way that demonstrates a clear understanding.

3.   Do the writing.

If you've ever stared at your computer screen, trying to think of something to write, I have good news for you. Because you've already established an outline, identified key topics, and developed a learning map, the actual writing should be a breeze. You already know what this paper is about and where it needs to go.

The most important part of any written assignment is the first paragraph. The first paragraph should always introduce the thesis and state the main topics. A poorly written start gives your professor little reason to read any further. The next most important element in your paper is your conclusion. The conclusion should summarize your topics and thesis into a few concise sentences. You should spend about 80 percent of your effort on the

The first paragraph should always introduce the thesis and state the main topics.

introduction and conclusion since 80 percent of your grade will be based on those two components.

Try to organize each topic within the body of your assignment, just like a mini essay, including an introduction, a body, and a conclusion.

Tip: Write your paper with an attention-grabbing introduction and an uplifting conclusion.

Paragraph Model

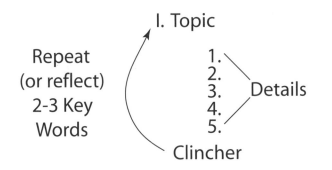

I. Topic

Repeat
(or reflect)
2-3 Key
Words

1.
2.
3. Details
4.
5.

Clincher

THINGS THAT ADD STYLE

Sentence openers are useful tools for developing effective style. Try to start each of your sentences with one. There are six basic types of sentence openers:

1. Subject
2. Prepositional
3. "-ly"
4. "ing" ("-ed")
5. Clausal (when, while, where, as, since, if, although, because)
6. VSS—a very short sentence (five words or less)

EXAMPLES OF SENTENCE OPENERS:

Subject	Accelerated Distance Learning is a quick and effective way to complete a degree program.
Prepositional	With Accelerated Distance Learning, you'll save countless hours that would have been spent in the classroom.
"-ly"	Shortly after starting an Accelerated Distance Learning program, you will begin to see dramatic results.
"-ing"	Using Accelerated Distance Learning, students can receive credit for real-life experiences.

Rather than attempting to crank out your assignment in a single sitting, break your writing time into smaller sessions.

Clausal	When you become an accelerated distance learner, the sky's the limit!
VSS	Learning is exciting!

THINGS THAT SLOW DOWN THE WRITING PROCESS

- **Starting at the beginning and trying to write straight through to the end.** Don't try to write sequentially—just write!

- **Expecting a sudden burst of inspiration that will bring the project together overnight.** Actually, this is nothing more than a formula for procrastination.

- **Doing it all at once.** Rather than attempting to crank out your assignment in a single sitting, break your writing time into smaller sessions. Spend an hour on your writing, take a break, and come back later for another hour. You'll find that you're much more creative and objective using this method.

- **Being overly meticulous with your first draft.** First, get your rough thoughts written out. Then, go back and polish up your grammar, usage, and style. (Editing is the sign of a good writer, not a bad one!)

THINGS THAT SPEED UP THE WRITING PROCESS

- **Learning to type and use a word processor.** If you don't already know how to type with a word processor, learn!

- **Using built-in electronic tools.** Your computer's spell-check, grammar-check, online dictionary, and thesaurus can help you proofread your work and find the words you need.

- **Using word lists.** Word lists such as an adverb list, preposition list, and strong verb list will help you write quickly and expressively. Lists of terms and phrases related to the subject you're writing about can also help. You can use a book's glossary or make your own lists as you study the subject.

- **Getting advice.** Discuss your writing project with someone else even before you begin writing. When you finish your draft, have it checked for stylistic consistency, logical flow, and organization. You may be blind to a flaw in your work that someone else might immediately spot.

- **Using "cut and paste."** Each time you write a paper, you do not need to type out your name, address, phone number, e-mail, student ID number, Social Security Number, course name, course number, and assignment number. Instead, cut and paste from other papers, create a macro, or use a template.

THINGS TO AVOID

- **Personal opinions.** Using *I think, I feel,* or *I believe* gives a childish quality to your writing and will make you appear unsure of the validity of your statements. Simply state the facts and support them with legitimate references. It is appropriate to speak of yourself and your opinions when sharing your personal experience, but reports and persuasive papers require concrete facts.

- **Word repeat.** Repeating words will aggravate most professors! Don't repeat a term unless it has major importance to your subject or is especially well-liked by your professor. Be creative and learn to use a thesaurus.

- **Losing your focus.** If it doesn't build toward your main points, don't include it!

- **Jumping around.** Your outline is what will keep you on track. If you're not following it, you're probably not presenting your ideas in the most logical order.

DOCUMENTATION

Good documentation impresses professors. Here are a few tips:

- **When to add references.** Don't interrupt your writing to insert references; make a note to add them later.

- **Order of references.** Never list more than two references in a row from the same source—it looks like you're plagiarizing.

- **Number of references.** Always provide at least two references more than required. Providing extra documentation shows the professor you're an especially diligent student and can help you earn an A.

- **Which statements need references.** Occasionally, professors challenged statements in my papers, but only when those statements weren't supported by a reference. Be sure your major points and assertions are firmly backed by good references.

- **Choosing references.** Because the world's base of information and knowledge is growing and changing so rapidly, you should make reference to recently published works as much as possible. Also, try to reference works that cover other topics you'll be writing about so you can use the same reference for more than one paper and more than one course.

- **Organizing references.** Create a separate electronic file with a list of all your references. Once you finish your paper, just cut and paste the references from your main list to the proper places in your paper. These stored references remain available for later writing assignments, eliminating the need to retype the information.

ONLINE RESOURCES

Many web sites offer advice on writing and let you link up with writing experts. Here are two you may find useful:

Online Writing Lab at Purdue University
owl.english.purdue.edu

Get your writing questions answered online.

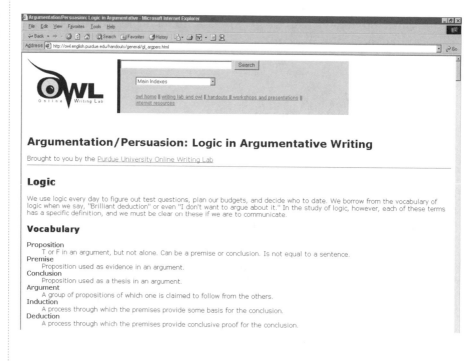

This site provides a wealth of information about writing for academic purposes: instructions for writing your term papers, information on writing style, and helpful hints on properly documenting your references.

APA and MLA style

webster.commnet.edu/apa/apa_intro.htm

webster.commnet.edu/mla.htm

This free, unofficial guide to APA and MLA styles gives good information and samples of the appropriate layouts so you can actually see the correct way to lay out your papers.

FROM THE EXPERT: *Attaining Excellence in Writing*

NAME: *Andrew Pudewa*

HOME STATE: *California*

COMPANY: *Institute for Excellence in Writing*

Because distance learning courses usually require the completion of even more writing assignments than traditional courses, it's critical that you learn to write well. Writing is an art, and like any other, this skill can be developed by copying the right models and having the right tools.

My goal in producing the video course, *Power Tips for Planning and Writing a College-Level Paper* was to help distance-learning students meet their need to quickly and effectively complete college assignments for a variety of subjects and a diversity of instructors. By using the writing methods from this course, you will be able to increase your confidence and competence, gradually developing your writing fluency. Learn to organize your topics, plan your papers ahead of time, and then write them stylishly by using a variety of sentence patterns. Don't think you can't. Outstanding college-level writing is something that everyone can achieve.

FINAL WORD

The tips in this chapter are simple and powerful. If you implement them, you'll be undaunted when faced with portfolios, course assignments, and essay exams.

I'd like to give special thanks to my friend, Mr. Andrew Pudewa, Director of the Institute for Excellence in Writing, whose suggestions for this chapter were a great help. I have learned much about writing from Mr. Pudewa, and now you can, too, through his tremendous *Advanced Communication Series*. See the *Student Success Catalog* for details.

Test-Taking Power:

Learning to Love the Challenge

13

"They know enough who know how to learn." —John Adams

My heart pounded. I gripped my pencil and answer sheet with sweaty palms as anxiety gripped my soul. It was the SAT fifth grade math test. "THINK, THINK, THINK, FASTER, FASTER!" In spite of my mental frenzy, I only continued to stare at the math problems in front of me. Fifty minutes later I handed in my half-finished answer sheet. I was devastated! Tears filled my eyes as I imagined how my future academic standing, personal worth, and entire future had been ruined by that terrible math test. Later, I recovered emotionally, but I developed a deep-seated hatred for all test taking.

Not until after high school when I learned the techniques of accelerated test preparation did my attitude toward tests change. Now, I actually look forward to the challenge because I know how to study for tests effectively and quickly.

PREPARING FOR TESTS SUCCESSFULLY

Just like a musician needs hours of careful practice before giving a performance, you must prepare diligently for exams. Test preparation is not particularly fun, but it pays off in the end. Since you'll be taking numerous tests, the relatively small amount of time that you will invest in learning the techniques of accelerated test taking will save you countless hours.

STEP 1: Learn about the exam.

Exams place more emphasis on certain test facts than others. Discover and focus on the most important facts. You should know:

- The course content that will be emphasized.

- The level of expertise required.

- The types of questions that will be asked (multiple-choice, true-or-false, essay).

- The types of essay answers expected, if any.

- How the test will be graded (how the answers are weighted).

Here's where to get that information:

YOUR TEACHER. Be tactful and respectful when you ask your teacher test-related questions.

TEST PREP BOOKS. Prep books like those published by Barron's, the Princeton Review, or The College Board can prove to be very handy resources in learning about tests.

SAMPLE EXAMS. Taking a sample test is usually a pretty accurate way to help you gauge how well you will do on the actual test.

TEST GUIDE SHEETS. Some testing programs provide these. They usually include a breakdown of the exam's content by percent. Knowing this information is critical to your success.

PREVIOUS EXAMS. Sometimes teachers are willing to hand them out.

STEP 2: Study.

We've already discussed the general principles of accelerated study in Chapters 9, 10, 11, and 12, so we'll skip ahead and talk about the final review.

STEP 3: Thoroughly review your notes and reading materials.

After finding out which areas of knowledge the test will focus on, do a final review of your studies, especially those most important parts. Go over your notes, both mental and paper. Look for new ways to organize them more effectively and reinforce the most important points in your memory.

Now, make a final review of your reading materials. Skim through the text and review the major points that were taught in each section. At this stage, you're mainly reading the book from memory, subconsciously reinforcing the material in your mind.

STEP 4: Memorize a final summary sheet.

Condense all the information you have gathered one more time. Organize it in a tidy package for easy recall: a single sheet of paper, a series of pictures or stories. Make sure that you have gathered the most essential and hard-to-remember material.

STEP 5: Take a mock test.

This is perhaps the most important and the most overlooked step. Studying for a test without taking a mock test is as foolish as a pianist practicing countless pieces of music without practicing the piece he's going to perform!

If the exam includes multiple-choice questions, try to get a sample test for practice. If it includes essay questions, make up your own sample questions based on the main topics in the course and practice writing out short essay answers.

You'll find that most tests place special emphasis on your understanding of specific terms related to the subject. I practiced writing these terms from memory and then used the terms to write mock test answers.

Take your final mock exam in a quiet place in order to aid concentration and more closely resemble the actual test conditions. This will help you determine how quickly you can answer the questions.

Take your final mock exam in a quiet place in order to aid concentration and more closely resemble the actual test conditions.

WHEN YOU GET TIRED OF TEST PREP—SIX REVITALIZERS

Studying for tests isn't easy. It is important that you maintain your focus and keep moving. For greater productivity, break your study periods into smaller time segments of one hour or less. For example, alternate between studying for forty minutes and resting for ten minutes. Develop a system that works for you and stick to it! Here are six things you can do during your breaks to refresh and renew yourself:

1. Relax your shoulders and let your arms hang loose. Concentrate on relaxing and breathing deeply for several minutes.

2. Take a brisk walk outside. Fresh air and a change of scenery will reenergize your brain.

3. Drink lots of water. Better than soft drinks and coffee, plain water will cleanse your body and improve your concentration.

4. Do some quick exercises—jumping jacks, push-ups, or sit-ups. I come up with some of my best ideas during these exercise sessions.

5. Eat a piece of fresh fruit for energy. Stay away from junk food.

6. Talk with someone about what you're learning. This two-way interaction can help you gain a new and fresh perspective on what you are studying.

STRATEGIC TEST TAKING

To score well on a test, you must know the material, but you must also know how to take tests. Many experts tout their "perfect strategy" for taking tests, but actually there isn't one perfect strategy. You are a unique person and will have a unique "perfect strategy" for approaching your tests. Some students prefer to start at the beginning of a test and move straight through to the end. Other students like to answer the hard questions first, while still others like to answer easy questions first. The four basic steps below are just that—basic. Only experimentation and practice on sample tests will help you determine what works best for you.

FOUR BASIC STEPS FOR PERFORMING YOUR BEST

1. READ THE DIRECTIONS. Don't assume that all tests are the same. They're not! Make sure you know the total number of questions, which (if any) carry greater weight, and the total time allotted for the test. Then you'll know how to budget your time.

2. SKIM OVER THE ENTIRE TEST BEFORE ANSWERING ANY QUESTIONS. Mentally note the type and difficulty of the questions as well as how much you know about them. If something you see triggers your memory, don't hesitate to jot down an important fact or formula that you'll need later. Skimming the test will help you see how the questions interrelate. Sometimes, by knowing that another question on the same topic will appear later in the test, you will have a better understanding of how to answer the question at hand.

3. ANSWER THE QUESTIONS. Analyze the question carefully to see what is really being asked; if you don't understand the question, don't waste time trying to think of an answer. Don't fall into the trap of spending most of your time on questions you know the least about: focus on what you know best and keep moving. Be sure to record your answers in the right place on the answer sheet.

4. GO BACK OVER YOUR WORK. Try to save ten to fifteen percent of your time for going back over questions you skipped. This would be the appropriate time to use the memory recall and effective guessing techniques described in the following pages. As a general rule, don't change your original answer to a question unless you have a compelling reason. Studies show that changing answers usually lowers the grade.

TIPS FOR MULTIPLE-CHOICE TESTS

- Beware of negatives. "No," "not," and "never," reverse the meaning of a question and may call for an opposite answer than your first impression.

- A choice with a superlative (such as "best," "greatest," or "most") is probably not correct.

- Don't waste time looking for trick questions.

- Answers that contain absolutes like "all," "always," "never," or "none" are usually wrong.

- If two answers are opposites, one of them is usually the correct answer.

- Answers that include the words "probably," "sometimes," or "some" tend to be right.

- Try to narrow your choices by eliminating wrong answers.

- Always make a guess if you can eliminate one of the choices.

- Watch out for answers that appear especially easy. Read the question again to see if you're missing something.

- If the question is very long or involves a passage that you have to analyze, read the choices for the answers before you read the question.

- Longer, more complicated answers are usually correct.

TIPS FOR TRUE OR FALSE TESTS

Here are a few additional things you should know about the true or false test.

- If you have the smallest clue, it is usually advantageous to guess even if there is a penalty for guessing.

- On true-or-false tests, long answers are often incorrect. The longer the answer, the more room for error.

- If you can think of just one good reason why the statement is false, it doesn't matter how many reasons there are why it might be right. The statement is false.

TAKING ESSAY EXAMS WITH EASE: WHAT YOU NEED TO KNOW

No matter how eloquent you write, if it's not legible, it may never even be read.

I used to hate essay tests, but now I prefer them over multiple-choice. With practice you can earn good grades more easily through essay tests than any other type of test. Essay questions allow for wide latitude in your answers, thus you will have a greater likelihood of being able to focus your answer on the areas you know best. So, learn to enjoy essay tests!

Here are some important pointers for you to remember when taking essay exams:

- Write legibly. Remember, what you write will be graded by a professor who will probably dislike having to strain his eyes to read your essay. No matter how eloquent you write, if it's not legible, it may never even be read.

- Analyze the question carefully for key words such as compare, criticize, discuss, illustrate, justify, and interpret. Let these specific instructions guide your writing.

- Be sure to spend enough time organizing your answer before actually beginning to write it out. Jot down an outline, using the key words of your essay. A good plan saves you time and helps present your ideas more coherently.

A good plan saves you time and helps present your ideas more coherently.

- Be concise. Avoid extra verbiage, eschew redundancy, and don't write excessively on one point!

- Focus on the facts. Don't spend too much time thinking of just the right word or making sure you have great style. Your ability to present factual information is what counts most on essay exams.

- Use appropriate terminology. This is your opportunity to demonstrate your learning. Effective use of the relevant terms shows superior understanding.

- State your thesis right away and don't hide it. It's the most important part of your essay.

- Pay special attention to your last paragraph. Next to your thesis, this paragraph will be the most noticed by your professor.

WHAT TO DO WHEN YOU CAN'T REMEMBER THE ANSWER

- Paraphrase the question. Try to state the question in your own words in order to clarify what is being asked.

- Think about things related to the question or what you think might be the answer. If the question asks you to name the first president of the U.S. and your brain freezes, think of things related to this person . . .Virginia, cherry tree, Revolutionary War, . . . Ah! George Washington!

- Write something down. Once you begin writing, the ideas will start to come.

- Save it for later. Skipping over a question and postponing your answer until later allows your brain to work subconsciously on finding the answer.

- Visualize it. Can you graphically construct something to represent the question? What pictures come to mind when you hear key words in the question?

- Look for clues in the wording of the question. You'd be surprised at how many times part of the answer is given right in the question or other questions on the test.

- Ask questions about the question. Do you know any information that is related to the question? Why is this question meaningful or important? How does this question relate to the subject as a whole?

PRACTICAL TIPS FOR SUCCESS ON TEST DAY

- Get plenty of sleep the night before the test. Fatigue diminishes your concentration and reduces your speed in taking the exam.

- Take one last skim. The last skim of the material you study in preparation for a test is the most important one. I recommend saving this review for the morning of the test because you'll be in better physical condition and the facts will be fresher in your mind.

- Dress comfortably. Dress in layers so you can adjust your clothing to the testing atmosphere.

- Bring what you need: number two pencils with good erasers, wristwatch, personal I.D., calculator, check for testing fee, and letter of authorization, if required. Bring duplicate equipment just in case. Dull pencils fill in answer sheet bubbles faster than sharp ones.

- Reject worry. When I took a foreign language test for which I didn't feel very prepared, I made a conscious decision not to think about the $200 cost or how important the outcome was to me. I kept reminding myself how much I enjoyed studying and communicating in this language. To my surprise, my score was higher than I ever dreamed of achieving!

THE SUCCESSFUL TEST TAKER

Prof said it wouldn't be easy, yet I remained confident. Although I'd spent less than a week studying for my final international economics test, I knew that my preparation had been thorough. I breezed through the questions in record time. "Explain the difference between Smith's principle of absolute advantage and Ricardo's principle of comparative advantage." No problem! "What is immiserizing growth?" Simple! The accelerated reading, memory, and test preparation skills I had learned really paid off. When the results came back, I had aced the exam. With these skills, you, too, can become a successful test taker!

PART IV

PUTTING IT TOGETHER

With the rock behind you, your anticipation grows for the final trails that will take you to Graduation Point. Your pace is faster than ever!

"Let's see," you think, pulling out your map. "Just two more ridges, and then I'll be reaching that waterfall." No surprises here. You studied this mountain range and mapped out your course long before hitting the trail. "After the waterfall, I'll come to Bald Ridge."

With a smile of anticipation, you fold your map neatly, tucking it into the map compartment on your backpack. Each piece of equipment you carry has a specific purpose, and you packed it logically for easy access. It is all in excellent working order and made of lightweight materials. Even your hiking boots are the best you could find, fitting your feet perfectly to avoid blisters.

You can hear the waterfall now, it is just ahead. Cresting the peak above the waterfall, you can see Bald Ridge. Right on course!

After Bald Ridge, Graduation Point is just a short distance away. Each step brings you closer!

Now that you understand the choices available to you through distance learning and the accelerated methods that will help you learn quickly, you still need a plan. Without a plan, you'll never be able to properly use your new tools for effectively earning your degree. Detailed and thoughtful planning will ensure that you don't get off course or become distracted. You'll know where you are headed and what to expect next in the process.

This is easier said than done. Finances, conflicting priorities, choosing the right school, goal setting—how can you make sense of it all? You have many choices to make as a distance learner, but rest assured, the answers you need are all in one place—right here. This section presents an easy-to-follow strategy that will help you accomplish all these objectives. It's the same strategy I used to earn my degree, and I'll show you how to adapt it so you can earn yours.

Choosing Your Path:

Finding the College That Fits You Best

14

Selecting the college where you will earn your degree is one of the single most important decisions in your pursuit of a degree. Don't rush. Use the following questions to analyze your choices.

IS THE SCHOOL ACCREDITED?

Today, anyone can go out and purchase what sounds like a legitimate credential, complete with a gold-embossed certificate recognizing their "graduation." Companies that promote their quick and easy way to get a diploma have become more aggressive in their advertising and have also become more suspect as being nothing more than "diploma mills." Employers are increasingly wary of such schemes and routinely conduct background checks evaluating the legitimacy of an applicant's degree and the institution they supposedly attended.

If you want your credentials to be recognized by a graduate program or provide you with the qualifications you need for a job, make sure you enroll in an accredited school. Accreditation should ensure that the school demonstrates fiscal responsibility, hires qualified teachers, and offers legitimate degree programs. Educators agree that accreditation is an important issue that deserves your careful attention.

If you choose an unaccredited school, you should have a clearly defined reason, such as the quality and type of instruction. For instance, some church- or denomination-sponsored schools maintain very high-quality programs but do not seek accreditation because of religious reasons.

Weigh the importance of accreditation for your future job and continuing education. If you're planning to spend your life serving refugees in Kenya, accreditation probably isn't very important; but if you want to attend graduate school at Harvard, accreditation is everything.

"Good fortune is what happens when opportunity meets with preparation."
—Thomas Edison

143

CHEA accredits the accreditors.

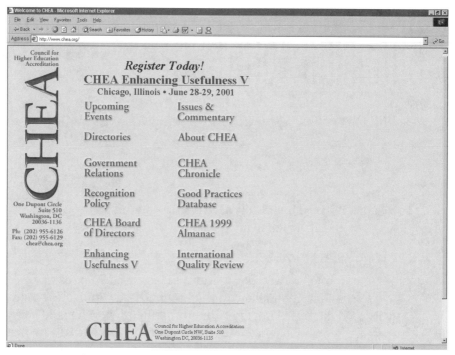

Beware though, not all accreditation is equal! There are four types of accreditation for colleges and universities.

REGIONAL ACCREDITATION. The six U.S. regional accrediting agencies are the most authoritative voice in accreditation. The Council for Higher Education Accreditation (CHEA) accredits all six regional accrediting agencies, thereby maintaining virtually identical standards among regionally accredited schools. Credentials that are acquired from schools that are not regionally accredited might not be accepted by another college or an employer.

STATE ACCREDITATION. Occasionally you will find an institution that has state but not regional accreditation. However, without regional accreditation you might have trouble transferring credits from one college to another. Ideally, your school will have both regional and state accreditation.

Credentials that are acquired from schools that are not regionally accredited might not be accepted by another college or an employer.

PROFESSIONAL ACCREDITATION. Professional accrediting agencies certify or accredit specific programs or courses that fall within a specific profession. For example, the Accreditation Board for Engineering and Technology (ABET) accredits engineering- and technology-related courses. Professional accreditation should be in addition to and not a replacement for regional accreditation. Professional accreditation is not always necessary—it just

DETC accredits distance-learning programs.

provides an even greater assurance that your training will be recognized as having been of the highest quality instruction.

Bogus Accreditation. Yes, there is such a thing! Some schools desiring to appear trustworthy and legitimate will set up an accrediting agency to accredit themselves. Who accredits these bogus accrediting agencies? Not the CHEA! Avoid these schools like the plague!

For a complete list of all the U.S. accrediting agencies, visit www.chea.org. Many of these are also listed in Appendix F.

DO I QUALIFY?

Before looking too closely at a particular school, first determine if you are even eligible to enroll. Some schools maintain an open enrollment policy, meaning they will accept and offer continuing enrollment to anyone who will maintain sufficient grades. However, most schools are very selective in their application process and have strict requirements. A college's requirements are usually listed on their application form, which is generally found in the student prospectus or the college's Web site. In applying, you might need to:

- Include a résumé, a list of references, and transcripts from previous schools or testing programs.

- Declare your choice of a major.

- Declare whether you are applying for financial aid.

- Take a standardized test.

- Write an essay.

Many colleges allow you to fill out an online application.

HOW MUCH IS TUITION?

Many students are fooled into thinking that the cost of their education also determines the quality of their education. In the world of academics, this just isn't true. A college's tuition is determined by the school's accreditation status and reputation, the type of institution (private, community, state, etc.), and the amount of government support it receives. For help in planning a tuition budget and reducing your tuition bill, see the next chapter.

WHAT COURSES ARE OFFERED?

Deciding beforehand what your major will be quickly narrows your search for a college, since a school that does not offer your major will not offer the courses that you'll need either. As you compare programs and courses between schools, look for those that place a special emphasis or have a well-known reputation in the major which you have chosen. These schools should have a better quality curriculum and a wider range of courses from which to choose for your degree program. You can find out which colleges are strong in your major from college catalogs, marketing materials, and third-party college guidebooks.

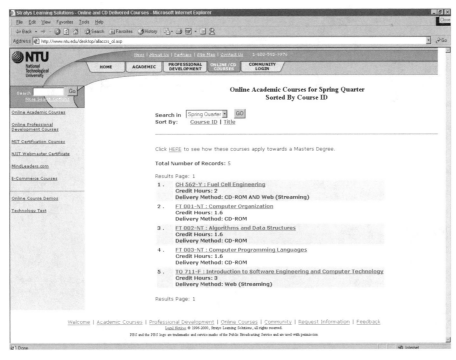

Check on type and availability of courses before enrolling.

Another consideration is the format of the courses offered by the school. The fact that two colleges offer courses with the same title doesn't mean what you learn and how you learn it will be the same at each school. One college's course might consist entirely of Web-based multimedia instruction, while another school might offer the same course through correspondence study completed through the mail.

The same course offered by two different schools will also vary in quality. Course quality depends on how the courses were developed, who teaches them, and what content is included. Sometimes you can examine a demo course before actually enrolling; check with the school's registrar.

WHAT ALTERNATIVE LEARNING METHODS ARE AVAILABLE?

Does the school accept portfolio assessment and credit earned through another school's examination program? Does the school offer independent studies? Will you be able to use courses from your local community college to fulfill certain course requirements? Verify ahead of time which methods will be allowed.

*College Web sites are
a great place
to begin your search
for the right school.*

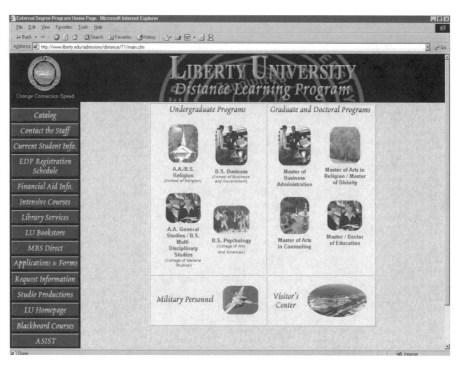

DOES THE SCHOOL CONSIDER ITS DISTANCE-LEARNING PROGRAM TO BE AN INTEGRAL PART OF THE SCHOOL?

*"Look before
you leap!"*

Unless the school is, in fact, emphasizing its distance-learning programs and allocating significant financial resources and expertise to their development, it is not serious about providing education at a distance. I chose Thomas Edison because I knew that distance education is its specialty. Go with a school that specializes in distance education, not one that merely pays it lip service.

HOW LONG WILL IT TAKE?

Some colleges operate on a very regimented schedule and will not allow the completion of a degree program in less than a minimum amount of time—usually four years for a bachelor's degree. Other schools are much more flexible, allowing credit through examination and portfolio assessment. Some will even allow students to accelerate their standard course work, provided they maintain satisfactory grades.

STUDENT'S POINT OF VIEW: *Course Quality Most Important in Choosing Your College*

NAME: *Ingrid Dahl*
HOME STATE: *Minnesota*
MAJOR: *Bachelor of Arts, Education*
COLLEGE: *Whitefield College*
AGE AT GRADUATION: *Currently enrolled*

When I realized that I needed more education to prepare for my future work, I completed several independent studies. Still, I wasn't sure how to bring my learning together into a unified educational pursuit. Then I found out about Whitefield College's distance-learning program.

Whitefield College offers degrees in Christian studies and provides students with a distinctly Christian approach to theology, philosophy, apologetics, history, psychology, and other related subjects. Because I wanted to work in Christian education, I knew that Whitefield would be an ideal choice for my higher education.

However, I also learned that Whitefield College has not sought government accreditation. So, before enrolling, I thoroughly scrutinized the school and its programs. I looked at the courses, examined the curriculum, and discussed the course construction and assignments with other students. I also visited the school's headquarters and spoke personally with the college faculty. Through this process I learned that Whitefield is committed to academic and theological excellence, requiring much more course work than most colleges.

So I enrolled, not worried about Whitefield's lack of state or regional accreditation, since solid Biblical course content was my chief goal. I found out that my degree will be honored by the Christian schools and mission boards with which I am interested in working, but, more importantly, I am confident that I am being properly equipped for a life of effective service.

The college's enrollment schedule will also significantly influence the amount of time it will take to complete a degree. Generally, enrollment opportunities are more flexible and frequent for distance learners. Some colleges will only enroll new students for the fall semester. Enrollment in specific courses might be available as often as every month or restricted to only once a year. Occasionally, you may find a course that allows for open enrollment—you can start whenever it is convenient for your schedule. These courses are the exception, not the rule.

The amount of effort required to complete a course will also vary greatly from school to school. Depending on the tests, course intensity, and number of assignments, study time can range from a couple of hours per week to full-time study.

Depending on the tests, course intensity, and number of assignments, study time can range from a couple of hours per week to full-time study.

Charter Oak has one of the most economical distance-learning programs.

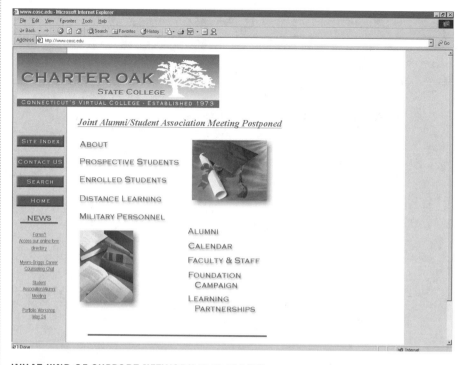

WHAT KIND OF SUPPORT NETWORK IS IN PLACE?

Evaluate the school's support network in the following areas:

ADVISORS. If you have questions about your degree program or certain course requirements, who will answer these questions? Ideally, you'll be assigned an advisor or mentor who specializes in your degree program. Will you be able to work with the same advisor on a regular basis? Working with the same person throughout your enrollment has obvious advantages.

DEPARTMENT OF TEST ADMINISTRATION. If the examinations for your course work will be proctored locally, what department within the school is responsible to mail these exams out on time and help you schedule your tests? Does this department have a direct phone number?

PORTFOLIO ASSESSMENT. While an increasing number of schools are accepting credit earned through portfolio assessment, there are very few that currently have well-developed programs, able to assess a broad range of portfolios. If you plan to rely heavily on this method of earning credit, make sure that the school you choose has a specialized department for assessing portfolios.

STUDENT COUNSELING CENTER/HELP LINE. If you have a simple question related to your degree-completion process, whom will you call for help? It is best if the school has an advising center or help line that you can call to get quick answers.

FROM THE EXPERT: *Tips for Success in Working With Your Advisor*

NAME: *Robert D. Herbster*
HOME STATE: *New Jersey*
POSITION: *Senior Program Advisor*
COLLEGE: *Thomas Edison State College*

In my fifteen years of experience advising students, I most appreciate students who are well prepared. Thomas Edison State College provides each student with a Program Planning Handbook that describes the student's relationship with the college and outlines the steps they need to take to successful degree completion. Students who make the effort to thoroughly read the handbook and other college material will, in the long run, fare better in completing their programs of study than those who do not. Advisors do not expect that students have memorized all of their planning material, but advisors do appreciate it when a student has made a strong effort to understand the process, as it indicates a high level of commitment from the student.

Some students may feel overwhelmed and be unprepared at the outset, but, with some guidance and encouragement from an advisor, students can get themselves squared away and on course. Completing a college degree is similar to taking a long trip. If you take the time to look at a map in advance, you will have a general understanding of where you are, where you are going, and how you are to get to your destination. Being prepared is certainly preferable to asking directions at every intersection.

Once a student has a general understanding of the program, the advisor assists the student in resolving any specific issues for which the student needs assistance. The student and the advisor each bring part of the solution to a particular issue. The advisor knows the policy of the college and all the possible ways of completing a requirement; the student knows his or her strengths and weaknesses and likes and dislikes. While the advisor can suggest the options available to solve a problem, ultimate responsibility rests with the student, who must decide which of the possible solutions is the most appropriate method based on the student's own background and abilities.

You can take courses from schools all over the world and later transfer those credits to the school where you are enrolled.

WILL I BE ALLOWED TO EARN CREDIT THROUGH MULTIPLE INSTITUTIONS?

In the new world of distance education, you are not limited to earning credit through only one institution. You can take courses from schools all over the world and later transfer those credits to the school where you are enrolled. Find out beforehand if the school you are thinking about enrolling in limits the type and amount of credit that may be transferred from other schools.

WHAT COLLEGES DO YOU RECOMMEND?

The college that's best for you really depends on your individual needs. There really isn't one distance-learning program that works for everybody. Decide on what's most important to you—course selection, choice of major, price, etc.—and look for colleges that offer what you want.

Here are a few colleges with which to begin your search. Learn about what's available, and then expand your search by checking on distance-learning programs in your home state where tuition is likely to be more reasonable.

Charter Oak State College
55 Paul J. Manafort Drive
New Britain, CT 06053
860-832-3800
www.cosc.edu

Excelsior College
7 Columbia Circle
Albany, New York 12203-5159
888-647-2388
www.excelsior.edu

Ohio University
Athens, Ohio, 45701
740-593-1000
www.ohiou.edu/lifelong

Thomas Edison State College
101 W. State St.
Trenton, NJ 08608-1176
888-442-8372
www.tesc.edu

University of Alaska Fairbanks
P.O. Box 757520
Fairbanks, AK 99775
907-474-7581
www.uaf.edu

HOW DO I GET ALL MY QUESTIONS ANSWERED?

Most of the information needed to make an informed decision about choosing a distance-learning provider is available online. Some schools even make their entire catalog available online, and those that don't will probably be glad to mail it to you at no charge.

Ohio University has a great selection of credit-earning options.

There is an incredible amount of information that is available—the problem is how to find it, quickly get answers to the most important questions, and objectively compare schools. The best way to find answers to these questions is to obtain a copy of *Peterson's Guide to Distance Learning*. This essential resource will answer the questions you have and will help you select the best school for your needs.

Selecting your school is one of the first steps in developing a strategy for completing your degree. It's an important decision that should be well thought out. The careful research that you do before making your selection will certainly pay off in the end.

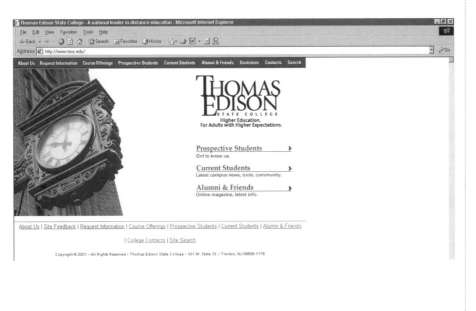

My alma mater.

Scholarships and Grants:

Calculating the Costs and Finding the Funds

Many young people wrongly assume that they can't afford a college education. With Accelerated Distance Learning, quality educational opportunities should be within the reach of every student.

There is surprisingly little correlation between the cost and the quality of education. Tuition and study materials may cost over $25,000 per year at many traditional private universities. In addition to the direct costs of tuition, fees, and books, there are also the indirect costs of transportation, housing, and meals. The total cost of a four-year program can easily reach $150,000. Compare these amounts with the $2,000 to $10,000 that you may spend for your entire degree program through distance education. Not only will the cost be less, but your education will be as good as, or even superior to, that of a traditional college. The quality of your education will only be limited by your own creativity, motivation, and diligence. Consider also the "opportunity costs" of the traditional route, all of the more meaningful things for which you could exchange your time: practical work experience, volunteer activities, world travel, and wages. The traditional college route takes too long and costs too much!

My degree from Thomas Edison cost less than $5,000, yet I would not trade my educational experience for four years at Harvard. I kept the price low by taking CLEP exams which cost less than $10 per credit. One comprehensive tuition fee allowed me to earn as many credits as I desired from Thomas Edison in a one-year period without paying addi-

More than fifty percent of recent college graduates leave school with over $10,000 to repay in student loans.

tional fees. (Paying a comprehensive fee rather than a per-course fee can save you a great deal of money.) In the end, my education cost about $40 per credit.

BASIC WAYS TO CUT THE COST OF COLLEGE:

1. Use credit-by-examination programs like CLEP to complete your first 30 credits.

2. Use less expensive online and independent study courses from your local community college to complete lower-level credits.

3. Use portfolio assessment for upper-level credits.

4. Enroll in a state college instead of a private university.

5. Pay a comprehensive tuition fee instead of paying a per course fee.

SHOULD I GET A LOAN?

More than 50 percent of recent college graduates leave school with over $10,000 to repay in student loans. Is this a good way to begin your career? Instead of going into debt for your education, I encourage you to spend only what you can afford.

If you must raise the money yourself, don't give up; many work opportunities are available to today's young person. I paid for my college tuition mostly with funds that I had earned from landscaping during my teen years.

FROM THE EXPERT: *Smart Financial Planning*

NAME: *Dan Pinkerton*
POSITION: *President of Pinkerton Financial Corporation and co-author of 21st-Century Wealth*

"I am thankful for the over $20,000 in scholarships and grants I received for college expenses. Yet, after I graduated from Stanford University, I still owed tens of thousands of dollars. My wife and I had to make huge sacrifices in order to pay off my debt. Later, we found out that I could have prepared much more effectively for my career in financial planning through distance learning. All of the top financial advisory school exams and every other required investment and insurance exam can be taken by correspondence. If only I had understood the principles of this book, I could have avoided some very costly mistakes. This book will be required reading for my six children."

Financial aid information is available through Charter Oak.

I'm so thankful for my grandpa's counsel to always deposit my earnings in a savings account right away. I earmarked those funds for future college expenses and earned extra money to pay my incidental expenses, rather than use my savings.

The financial aid system penalizes students that have significant personal assets.

If your parents or others are planning to help you with college expenses, it is wise to not transfer those funds into your name until absolutely necessary. The financial aid system penalizes students that have significant personal assets. When the financial aid assessment is made, the money that is kept in your account will reduce your available aid and be penalized at approximately 35%, whereas, the money in your parents' account will be penalized at approximately 6%. How you structure things can make a big difference in how much financial aid you receive.

If your parents want to finance a very expensive education for you, consider asking them to save this money until after you finish your degree. At that point, you could use those funds for more education, a house, or starting your own business.

FINDING SCHOLARSHIPS AND GRANTS

There are many sources for assistance with college tuition, and you don't have to be poverty-stricken to qualify. Every year, more than twenty-thousand private, corporate, and school agencies give away billions of dollars in scholarships.

If you have already picked your college, go to its Web site for information about getting financial aid.

Most schools use what is called an Expected Family Contribution (EFC) to decide how much financial aid you can receive. Your EFC is calculated by the federal government when you complete a form called the Free Application for Financial Student Aid (FAFSA). You can fill it out online at www.fafsa.ed.gov. Two to four weeks after you complete the form, you will receive your official student aid report from the government, containing your EFC calculation. There are several different types of Federal grants for which you can apply through the FAFSA. Your college should inform you as to which ones you qualify for.

State grants are offered mostly to state residents and may require that you attend an in-state school. For information on how to contact state student grant agencies, go to www.students.gov/states.cfm.

Every year, more than twenty-thousand private, corporate, and school agencies give away billions of dollars in scholarships.

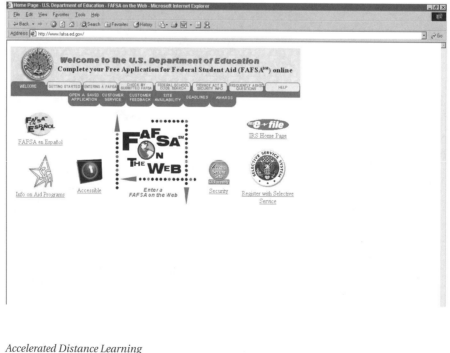

Complete your FAFSA on the Web.

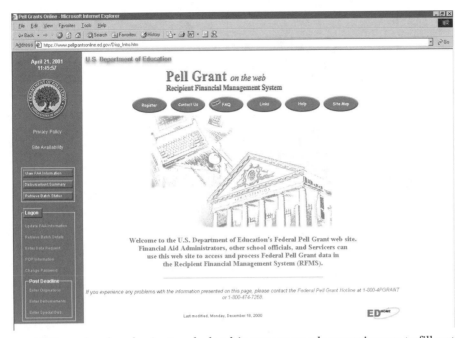

Grants and scholarships are available for distance-learning students too.

Many school and private scholarship programs also require you to fill out a CSS/Financial Aid PROFILE. This is a program administered by the College Board. To fill out the CSS profile online, go to www.collegeboard.org/finaid/fastud/htm/proform.html. Have your credit card handy so you can pay the $6 registration fee and the $16 application delivery fee for each school or scholarship program to which you want to apply.

Here are a few Web sites that will help you find scholarships for which you are eligible.

COLLEGE-SPECIFIC SCHOLARSHIPS:

MeritMoney

www.meritmoney.com

MeritMoney provides the only existing searchable database of academic scholarships available from the colleges and universities themselves. If you have a 3.0 GPA or higher and want to find out which colleges may have academic scholarships (free money) for you, visit MeritMoney.com. (They will also show you how much additional free money could be available from the colleges if you improve your SAT/ACT score—a great motivational tool!)

Tip: While calculating trip expenses is important, it's the hike that really matters; concentrate on your study, not money.

Merit Money—a database of academic scholarships available from the colleges and universities.

They do charge a small fee, but it's worth it to get access to their unique and extensive database. Use Promotion Code DL25 to receive a 15% discount on the membership fee.

PRIVATE/CORPORATE SCHOLARSHIPS:

FastWeb

fastweb.com

FastWeb provides the largest searchable database of private and corporate scholarships. Their service is free and already has over two million registered users. After you fill out an online application, FastWeb provides you with a list of scholarships that match your student profile.

COLLEGE BOARD SCHOLARSHIP

http://apps.collegeboard.com/cbsearch_ss/welcome.jsp

This site works like FastWeb and might turn up scholarships that Fast-Web missed.

REDUCING YOUR TAXES

Two federal tax credit programs can make your education more affordable. The Hope Credit can be worth up to $1,500; the Lifetime Learning

Credit, up to $2,000. For more information, go to http://www.irs.gov/newsroom/article/0,,id=107670,00.html.

FINDING THE BOTTOM LINE: FIGURING THE TOTAL COST

Now that you have an idea of how much financial aid you'll be able to receive, fill out the chart below to estimate your college expenses.

COLLEGE BUDGET SHEET			
ITEM	COST	QUANTITY OR NUMBER OF CREDITS	TOTAL
Application Fees			
a. College A's cost per credit			
a. College B's cost per credit			
a. College C's cost per credit			
b. Cost per credit for credit-by-examination program 1			
b. Cost per credit for credit-by-examination program 2			
b. Cost per credit for credit-by-examination program 3			
c. Telecommunications charges			
Textbooks and study materials			
Postage			
Graduation Fee			
d. Other			
e. Grants and scholarships (subtract)			
Total Cost of Degree			$ _____

a: You'll probably take courses from several different schools and transfer credit to the college from which you graduate.

b: List any individual examination programs like CLEP, DANTES, and AP that you plan to take.

c: Long-distance phone calls, Internet connection, and college telecommunications user fees.

d: Will you need to make a trip to the school campus? Will you have to upgrade your current computer system? Enter these costs here.

e: Subtract the amount of financial aid you expect to receive.

f: The final cost of your entire degree program will be much less than you initially thought.

MAINTAINING YOUR FOCUS

Calculating the costs of your college education and finding additional sources of funding is a necessary step, but don't spend too much time on this process. Consider what the real financial return is on your investment of time. Sometimes, earning the money you need is faster than finding student aid! Go ahead and quickly fill out the college cost sheet (previous page), get your EFC online, apply for a Pell Grant, and try an online scholarship search, but don't waste time chasing every $25 scholarship. You still have a long trail to hike and many mountains to climb!

Maximum Efficiency: 16

Organizing Yourself and Your Surroundings

O rder study materials for your course in Macroeconomics. Set up an independent study with a local professor. Turn in your last paper and take the final exam in Business Ethics. Plus, stay on top of all of life's routine responsibilities! Accelerated Distance Learning is only possible when you're highly organized. Sometimes, getting organized is a complex task in itself. You will need to master the art of establishing priorities, sticking to a schedule, and building good habits. Here is an essential list of what you need to do:

"Good order is the foundation of all good things."
—Edmund Burke

- Know the tasks and the best times to do them.
- Create a "to-do today" notebook and use it daily.
- Arrange your study area for efficiency and comfort.
- Stay focused.
- Save time and energy by using synergy.
- Arrest time robbers.
- Maintain a sound body for a sound mind.
- Continually monitor your efficiency.

Let's look closer at each of these crucial areas.

KNOW THE TASKS AND THE BEST TIMES TO DO THEM

The life of an accelerated distance learner is essentially composed of the following tasks:

- Planning your courses—enrolling, ordering study materials, scheduling tests.
- Conducting online research.
- Accessing library resources.

- Creating special learning activities such as internships and portfolios.
- Reading textbooks.
- Using audiovisual and multimedia resources.
- Writing assigned papers.
- Communicating with faculty members and students.
- Returning assignments.
- Taking exams.
- Eating.
- Resting.
- Exercising.

Some of these tasks are more demanding than others and require special concentration and creativity. For instance, writing an assignment takes much more effort than reading a textbook. You must first distinguish between the difficult and easy tasks and then arrange your schedule so that you do the hardest tasks first thing every day. Your schedule might look something like this:

7:30–12:00	Do writing assignments and related research.
12:30–3:00	Read assigned materials for courses.
3:00–4:00	Do online research and study projects.
4:00–5:00	Make telephone calls and handle e-mail.
6:00–9:00	Read more assigned materials.

CREATE A "TO-DO TODAY" NOTEBOOK AND USE IT DAILY

Consider not only the difficulty of a task, but also its importance. Writing an e-mail to your professor is more important than talking on the phone to a friend. Prioritize the items on your "to-do today" list and do them in order of importance. Always!

Here's why you need a "to-do today" list:

- To help you evaluate which tasks are most important.
- To put more important tasks before less important ones.
- To track your progress as you check off completed activities and evaluate those that remain.

"Procrastination is the father of failure."
—Elbert Hubbard

In addition to a "to-do today" list, you should have "to-do this week," "this month," and "this year" lists. You should be able to see how your present activities fit into your overall plan. When I started completing my degree program, I began using a monthly planner. I wrote in all the important dates for the entire year: when courses would begin and end, when I planned to take certain tests, and how long I would spend studying certain subjects. I often had to move things around, but putting all this information on paper helped me set my goals and gauge my progress.

Scheduling programs such as *Microsoft Outlook* do have some timesaving features, but they should not be considered a necessity; paper and pen will do.

The two biggest and most important tasks you face as an accelerated distance learner are preparing for tests and completing writing assignments. For tasks of this magnitude, it's not enough to just write down the name of the course on your schedule. You need to specifically outline how you will complete it. For example:

1.   Write 500 words of assignment.
2.   Outline next section of assignment.
3.   Read pages 253–398 of assigned text.
4.   Review material read yesterday.
5.   Identify important course concepts for upcoming test.
6.   Do mock test in preparation.

Before you go to bed each night, prepare the next day's "to-do" list so that your brain will subconsciously think through and prepare for the coming tasks.

ARRANGE YOUR STUDY AREA FOR EFFICIENCY AND COMFORT

For maximum effectiveness, your study area should be as quiet and distraction-free as possible. A separate room just for study is not necessary; I used my bedroom. My family cooperated by keeping the noise down in the surrounding area.

Keep everything necessary for your work in your study area. This includes your computer, printer, telephone, bookshelf, writing supplies, and file box. Having to take a "hunting trip" away from your work area will waste time.

Put first things FIRST!

"Have a time and place for everything, and do everything in its time and place, and you will not only accomplish more, but have far more leisure than those who are always hurrying, as if vainly attempting to overtake time that had been lost."
—Tyron Edwards

STUDENT'S POINT OF VIEW: *Organization Results in Efficiency*

NAME: *Alexandra Swann*
HOME STATE: *Texas*
DEGREE: *Bachelor of Arts, Master of Arts*
COLLEGE: *Brigham Young University and California State University*
AGE AT GRADUATION: *16*

Distance education was a very positive experience for me, but it required hard work. For example, to earn my bachelor's degree, I wrote 120 papers (the shortest was 500 words) and a fifty-page thesis. Plus, after I completed each major component of my degree I spent two weeks on campus studying under my professor, taking tests, and meeting other students.

Distance learning allows a student to earn a degree more quickly. Rather than sitting in class for six hours a week for a semester to earn one set of credits, I just finished a fixed number of assignments. As soon as I finished one assignment, I started the next. Consistency was critical to the success of this home-study program. I couldn't miss days and then try to catch up later. I completed my studies quickly because I made them a priority and stayed on schedule. As a result, I completed my bachelor's degree in two-and-a-half years without skipping or testing out of any subject. Likewise, I earned my master's in eighteen months, graduating in 1987 at the age of sixteen. The total cost for both degrees was just $8,000!

Distance learning does not subject the student to the college lifestyle. For example, I never had to face the temptation to attend wild parties. This is the greatest benefit of distance learning—an exceptional education, free of moral compromise.

Alexandra Swann is the author of No Regrets: How homeschooling allowed me to earn my Master's degree by age 16.

Here are a few tips for setting up your study area:

- COMPUTER SCREEN. Place it just close enough to you to be able to read it. The closer the monitor is to you, the greater the strain on your eyes.

- DESK. My monitor is the only thing on my large desk which leaves plenty of space for me to spread out my textbooks, study guides, notes, and writing projects. The PC tower sits under the table, and my keyboard rests in a sliding tray attached to the underside of the table.

- **CHAIR.** When you're sitting, the angle between your upper legs and spine should be 90°. If you're typing, your elbow angle should be 90° also. Your feet should comfortably reach the floor. A spare kitchen chair usually doesn't suffice; visit your local office supply store and examine their chairs with adjustable seat heights and backrest positions. You may also need to adjust the height of your table or get a footrest. Any expenditures for study comfort will be money well spent.

- **FILE BOX.** Yes, you should have your own. A simple plastic file box provides a separate place to store college catalogs, returned test scores, and completed research projects.

- **YOURSELF.** Don't hunch over, always sit erect, keep your feet firmly planted on the floor, and change position periodically.

- **TELEPHONE.** Put it next to your computer so you can type and talk at the same time. Because you'll be using the phone a lot, you might want to get a second line installed or subscribe to DSL.

- **BOOKSHELF.** Mine is right next to my desk so that I can reach all the books I need for my studies. I group the books I am studying together so I can find them easily.

STAY FOCUSED

Here are a few tips on how to avoid distractions:

- Don't take phone calls during your most intense study periods. They shatter concentration which is necessary to achieve creative "flow" when writing and maximum retention when studying. Establish a block of time in your day when you are free from all interruptions.

- Don't socialize on the phone or Internet during study time. Communicating and collaborating with others is great, but keep this communication focused on the subject you're studying.

- Stay close to home. Every minute spent traveling is a minute that could have been spent studying. Try to find what you need online and use resources like libraries and test centers that are in your area.

- Don't check e-mail all day. Check e-mail once or twice a day, preferably near the end of the day. Schedule enough time to respond immediately to e-mail so you only need to read it once.

Focus on your major objectives.

"Always at it wins the day." —Proverb

- Organize your papers. Separate the papers that come across your desk into categories: research papers, writing assignments, degree audits, etc.

- Multitask. For example: listen to lecture tapes in the car, mentally review subject outlines while unloading the dishwasher, read a book while standing in line, or mentally plan the day while exercising.

SAVE TIME AND ENERGY BY USING SYNERGY

There will usually be duplication in the content of some of the courses you take, especially in the more specialized courses. Studying similar courses at the same time increases your study speed and effectiveness. While I was preparing to take "Principles of Management," I noticed that "Human Resources Management" covered very similar content. I took both courses at the same time and experienced synergy in my studies. Concepts learned in one course made the content of the other course easier to understand. The new vocabulary that I memorized was applicable to both courses.

Because you are an independent learner, you aren't fixed to the schedule of a school or professor—you can organize your own course schedule for the greatest synergy. Start making synergy work for you!

ARREST TIME ROBBERS!

Life brings with it a multitude of mundane tasks: cleaning the house, taking out the trash, washing dishes. Don't despise these little things, but at the same time don't allow them to control your life. Work out a plan with your family for sharing responsibilities. Try to group your tasks into consolidated time segments so you can do them all at once, rather than suffer continual interruptions while you're studying.

"I find television very educating. Every time somebody turns on the set, I go into the other room and read a book."
—Groucho Marx

You should also set aside many of the activities you do "just for fun." Playing sports, attending parties, and aimlessly surfing the net may be enjoyable, but they won't move you any closer to the completion of your major objective.

For many people, the greatest time thief is television. You probably don't realize how much of your time this device consumes every week. If you want news reports, it's far more effective to get them in print or online. Videos can also be a waste of time. When I was pursuing my degree, I only watched half of one video that was unrelated to my studies. Why stare at a video when you could be speeding toward your degree?

While the issues I have addressed here are very simple, they should not be taken lightly. Recently, I talked with a discouraged young man who "could not find time" to complete his degree. It wasn't that he didn't have time. He let little things eat up his time—there was a concert in town that he just *had* to go to, his garage needed to be reorganized, a friend called to go out to lunch . . . . Don't let this happen to you!

MAINTAIN A SOUND BODY FOR A SOUND MIND

To function at full capacity you must take care of your body. This means regular exercise, a healthy diet, and enough sleep. Here are some practical suggestions:

- Eliminate sugar, alcohol, cigarettes, caffeine, aspartame, white flour, and soft drinks from your life! Start reading labels.

- Eat more raw vegetables. Raw foods contain enzymes and vitamins that can't be obtained from processed foods. When my family first made a change in our diet and began eating less meat, I thought I would starve. Instead, I began feeling more energetic! The processed foods I had been eating were routing the blood from my brain to my stomach and robbing me of the ability to concentrate. If I limit my food intake to fruit or vegetable juice before a test, my brain stays much more alert and focused. My sisters wrote a cookbook to help people begin a healthier lifestyle. Check out the *Student Success Catalog* for details.

- Exercise regularly. The key word is *regular*. Inconsistent exercise is practically a waste of time. Aerobic exercises such as jogging, swimming, or jumping on a trampoline strengthen your heart. Anaerobic exercise (lifting weights) strengthens your other muscles. You don't have to be muscular to lift weights. My own exercise program is very simple. It consists of first doing some push-ups and sit-ups, followed by using a set of hand weights for upper body exercise. After jumping on the indoor trampoline to get my heart rate going and some stretching to loosen up tight muscles, I'm ready to tackle my studies.

- Stretch. Long hours of study can put a lot of stress on your back and neck. I learned this the hard way. After several months of pouring over books, the muscles on the back of my neck became inflamed. However, once I incorporated exercises into my routine that stretched these muscles, the inflammation quickly disappeared and never returned. Just a few minutes of stretching goes a long way toward preventing injury.

- Schedule sleep. Regular times for going to bed and getting up are much better for your body than an irregular sleep schedule.

MAINTAINING FAMILY HARMONY

One of the main reasons I succeeded in getting a degree was the constant support and understanding of my family. We worked out a plan together which achieved all of our goals. Here are a few tips you should discuss with your family:

- Create mutual understanding. Explain to your family your desire to obtain a degree and make sure you have their support.

- Maintain lines of communication. Regularly discuss how things are working out and identify improvements that can be made to your schedule and responsibilities.

- Involve your family in your learning. Do you need to do some research at the museum? Take a family member along. Are you required to watch a video? Watch it with the family. Are you writing papers? Get the family to review them. Be creative!

- Establish "quiet times." Set apart a time during the day that is free from interruptions and use it for your most intensive and demanding study.

- Keep your clutter to a minimum. Don't tempt others to secretly "help" you clean it up.

- Create computer usage guidelines. Will others in the family be using your computer? Establish guidelines for moving and deleting files, installing software, and scheduling time on the computer.

CONTINUALLY MONITOR YOUR EFFICIENCY

Never become content with how you work and study. Continue to rigorously scrutinize your work patterns like an efficiency expert, repeatedly asking yourself, "Is there a better way?"

Each of us receives only twenty-four hours to do our daily work and study. Time is your most precious resource, and how you use it will inevitably determine the speed of your progress. You'll be amazed at how much work you will be able to accomplish as you stay focused on your major objective!

Getting organized needs to become a top priority. When things are in their proper place, and you are able to operate efficiently, you will feel more relaxed and excited about the total learning process.

"Know the true value of time; snatch, seize, and enjoy every moment of it. No idleness; no laziness; no procrastination; never put off till tomorrow what you can do today."
—Lord Chesterfield

Mapping a Course:

A Strategy for Your College Success

17

If you were going on a thirty-day hike, would you plan your route before you left? Of course! Do the same in your pursuit of a degree. Making specific plans before starting your journey will save an incredible amount of time. Lack of planning ensures failure.

The following steps are critical to your degree-completion process. Don't be concerned about the order in which you complete them; however, make sure that you address each area.

1. **Discover your life purpose.**

Before you begin working toward a degree, do some serious soul-searching. How will this degree enhance your leadership qualities? How will it assist you as you seek to benefit the lives of others? How does it fit into your long-range plan? Answering these questions first will make the degree-completion process much more meaningful.

2. **Get organized.**

Begin implementing the tips on organization explained in Chapter 16. Prepare now and you'll streamline your studies while avoiding future frustration.

3. **Develop accelerated learning skills.**

Begin by spending one or two solid weeks mastering accelerated learning techniques before jumping into the actual studies. Order the accelerated learning tools in the *Student Success Catalog* so you can get started immediately. Accelerated learning skills will form the foundation for all of your learning.

4. **Prepare your funding.**

You probably won't know exactly how much grant and scholarship money you'll be eligible to receive until you enroll in a school. However,

"Great minds have great purposes, others have wishes."
—Washington Irving

Principle #10: MOTIVATION. The true success of any achievement will be proven by the presence or abscence of proper motivation.

173

since your college education will obviously require some personal expense, start saving now. To estimate your tuition cost, multiply the number of credits you need times the average cost per credit. Review Chapter 15 for more information on how to make this estimate.

5. CHOOSE YOUR MAJOR.

What's your destination? Do you want to complete a degree in computer science, business, or nursing? It is not necessary to choose a major before starting to earn credit, but you will have to select a major before planning your degree-completion schedule.

See Appendix C for a comprehensive list of majors available through distance learning.

6. CHOOSE YOUR COLLEGE.

Even if you don't actually enroll in a college now, decide on which college you will enroll in so you will know which courses will be required for your degree. Collect college catalogs and watch for courses that will fit into your degree program. When you finally enroll in the college of your choice, you will probably take courses offered by other schools as well, depending on their availability, cost, and quality.

7. ESTABLISH YOUR GOALS.

Type of learning: What kind of learning experience do you want? Do you want to get credit for prior learning experiences, or do you want to study material that is completely new to you? What topics will be most valuable for you to study?

Grades: Determine what grades you will be satisfied with or need on individual courses and what GPA you need to achieve. Are you planning to enroll in a graduate school after finishing your undergraduate studies? What are the entrance requirements for admission?

Timing: How long do you want your studies to take? If you're ready to put everything else in your life on hold, you could easily earn your degree in less than a year, as I did. Or, you can do more standard course work and finish in a couple of years.

8. CHART OUT YOUR DEGREE PROGRAM.

You have several distance-learning methods from which to choose: testing, portfolio, independent study, and online courses. Furthermore, within each method there are additional choices, such as choosing which exams to take or what experiences to put in a portfolio. The path you choose will be as unique as you are; with Accelerated Distance Learning, no two degree programs are the same. Start by filling out a Degree-Completion Worksheet, as explained at the end of this chapter. This is an absolute must if you plan to complete your bachelor's degree in less than a year.

9. REVISE YOUR PLAN WITH AN ADVISOR.

After you fill out your Degree-Completion Worksheet, send it to your advisor for advice and approval. It's possible that you selected a course that is unsuitable for completing your degree requirements. Remember, your advisor can tell you what a course will involve, but only you can decide if you want to take it. Be creative in thinking of alternate ways to meet course requirements and then go to your advisor for approval. Regularly inform the advisor of your current study activities and progress.

Sometimes, students must make appointments with academic advisors several weeks in advance, so plan ahead.

10. MAKE A SCHEDULE.

Break up your goal of getting a degree into bite-sized pieces, such as individual courses and tests. Then, plug the pieces into your calendar. Leave some slack for the inevitable interruptions that life brings, but don't underestimate the speed at which you can learn using accelerated learning techniques.

As I planned how I would complete my degree, I decided to try to get all 120 credits in six months, which meant that I needed to earn about five per week. I wasn't sure I'd be able to work that fast, but by using the techniques in this book, I was able to complete up to nine credits a week. In the end, I finished in less than six months with 129 credits.

Your speed will depend on which distance-learning methods you use. I found that credit-by-examination was the fastest way to earn credits. On average, I needed ten to twenty hours to prepare for a test. Because most tests are three credits each, I could easily earn six credits per week by taking exams. Your preparation time will depend on the difficulty of the subject and your familiarity with it.

Portfolio credit is probably the second easiest to earn. It took me about a week to write a narrative and collect supporting documentation for a three-credit portfolio. If you take online or correspondence courses, plan to spend at least fifty hours on each course. Because you have to send assignments back and forth and wait for your grades, each course will take several weeks. That's why I liked working on three correspondence courses at once.

Remember these time estimates when you plan how long it will take to complete your degree. If you hope to finish in less than six months, you'll probably rely pretty heavily on credit-by-examination. If you find that you need to use more traditional course work, it will take longer to complete your degree.

My calendar page from March 2000. It was a challenge, but I stayed on schedule because I broke the process into small steps.

Brad's Study Calendar - March 2000						
S	**M**	**T**	**W**	**T**	**F**	**S**
			1 FIN-230 DANTES Test	2 Setup Independent Study BUS-220	3 Begin Studying COM-340	4 COM-340 Papers 1&2
5	6 FIN-334 Study	7 COM-340 Study	8 COM-340 Paper 3	9 COM-340 Paper 4	10 Review	11 COM-340 Test
12	13 COM-340 Review & Self Test	14 COM-340 Paper 5&6	15 COM-340 Final Test	16 Review FIN-334	17 FIN-334 Test	18
19	20 Reasearch For Portfolio	21 Collect Evidence	22 Begin Writing Portfolio	23 Write Narrative	24 Write Narrative	25 Write Narrative
26	27 Write Narrative	28 Submit Portfolio	29 TRAN-217 Study	30 TRAN-217 Study	31 TRAN-217 Paper 1	

Here are some tasks you should include on your calendar:

- **Registering for courses.** Plan in advance. They do fill up!
- **Assignment completion**
- **Course completion.** When are your papers and/or exams due?
- **Tests**
- **Appointments with your advisor.** Schedule these often.
- **Ordering course materials.** Order materials from your library or text-book suppliers ahead of time.

Look ahead at the whole degree-completion process and jot down everything on your calendar. Sure, your plan will change, but this process will help you see how everything is going to fit.

11. STUDY ACCORDING TO PLAN.

Once you pick a course or exam, estimate how long it will take you to prepare. Then, divide that time into specific study segments. When I took the CLEP exams for Micro and Macroeconomics, I only scheduled four days for

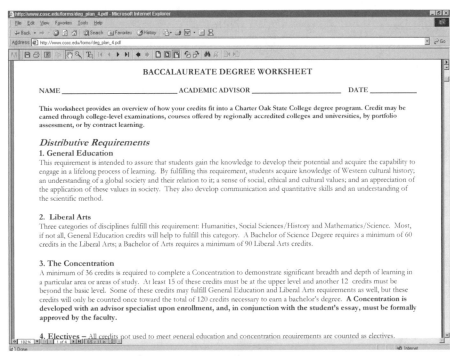

A college's program planning sheet lets you know what courses you'll need to take.

study and preparation. I had 1,500 pages to read, so I decided to spend three days speed-reading and use the fourth day to review the material several times. My score was in the ninety-eighth percentile.

12. REVISE YOUR PLAN.

In distance learning, you set the pace and choose your course of study. Your plan should provide structure and enable you to set goals but also be flexible enough to change with your needs.

13. KEEP GOING.

Now that you've broken down your goal into daily assignments, be determined to stick with the plan! Certainly, there will be challenges along the way. During the difficult times, be ready to step back from your studies for a moment and consider how even these challenges may relate to your life purpose. During times of discouragement, I would look at the map of China hanging on my wall. I would think of my experiences there, the people I had met, and how much I wanted to help them. Suddenly, my resolve to complete my degree would return.

Tip: The secret is to keep moving.

AN OVERVIEW OF THE TYPICAL DEGREE PROGRAM

Before you start planning your own degree program, let's look at the typical program's structure and requirements. Most baccalaureate degrees require completion of 120–128 semester credits in four years. Most degree programs can be divided into the following three components:

1.   GENERAL EDUCATION OR LIBERAL ARTS REQUIREMENTS. The first 36–60 credits of a degree program consist of general courses in English, general education, mathematics, arts, and sciences.

2.   AREA CONCENTRATION. This consists of a series of core courses and a specialization within those courses. Business administration students would complete a core of business subjects such as economics, marketing, finance, and business law. They would also complete a specialization within that core of business requirements. A student specializing in human resources management would take a number of courses like organizational behavior, organizational development, and organizational change to complete this part of his degree.

3.   FREE ELECTIVES. This component of your degree can be filled with just about anything that interests you.

A specified number of your credits must come from upper-level courses (300 or 400 series) versus lower-level courses (100 or 200 series). You must also meet one or more "depth requirements," which means completing a significant number of credits within one subject area. Your specialization is one example of this, and you may very well have additional depth requirements.

It's very important to make sure a course or examination will fit into your degree plan before you take it.

YOUR MAP FOR COLLEGE SUCCESS: Filling Out Your Degree-Completion Worksheet

Ok, grab a paper and pencil and start writing out your own map. Here's how:

1.   Decide on a major.

2.   Choose a college that offers your major.

3.   Get a copy of the college's course catalog online or by mail.

4.   Look up the credit distribution requirements for your degree program.

5. Locate the information that outlines the credit distribution requirements for your concentration/specialization.

6. Discover and list acceptable alternatives (courses, tests, and portfolio options) for each credit requirement.

7. Fill out the Degree-Completion Worksheet (see Appendix D).

8. Later, after enrolling, send your completed worksheet to your advisor and revise it as needed.

SAMPLE MAPS OF THREE ACCELERATED DISTANCE LEARNERS

Before you start filling out your Degree-Completion Worksheet, examine the following worksheets of three actual students with various levels of experience and maturity. Seeing their completed sheets and the choices they have made may help you understand the entire process better.

The following Degree-Completion Worksheets are quite similar to the one that you will produce. These plans are meant to introduce you to the process of outlining a degree-completion plan and are by no means exact models for you to copy. These tentative plans will only become official after an advisor approves all of the courses. Each plan is in a slightly different format, due to the differences in the schools and the degrees being pursued.

It is usually very easy to determine which lower-level credits will be needed. Students who begin completing these courses before actually enrolling in a college are generally able to reduce their overall tuition expense. However, before you start taking classes in the area of your specialization, work with an advisor to make sure that you are on the right track.

Sixteen and Just Getting Started: David Voeller

Computers, woodworking, business, art, music—these are just a few of David Voeller's many interests. These aren't just passing interests either. David really pours himself into a subject and learns all he can about it. With so many interests, why spend four years confined in a classroom focusing on only one subject?

By taking one to two exams every month, David plans to complete all the general education requirements and quite a few business and computer credits. Later, he'll work with an advisor to plan the smaller, more specialized component of his degree. But for now, David knows he has a plan for making steady progress toward his degree. Because David will earn most of his credits through credit-by-examination, his degree should cost less than $4,000.

Before you start taking classes in the area of your specialization, work with an advisor to make sure that you are on the right track.

> "Perseverance and tact are the two great qualities most valuable for all men who would mount, but especially for those who have to step out of the crowd."
> —Benjamin Disraeli

STUDENT'S POINT OF VIEW: *Maximum Opportunity and Focus for Studies*

NAME: *David Voeller*
HOME STATE: *Illinois*
MAJOR: *Bachelor of Science, Information Systems*
COLLEGE: *Charter Oak State College*
AGE AT GRADUATION: *Enrolling soon*
CURRENT AGE: *16*

My enthusiasm for distance learning continues to grow as I realize the tremendous opportunity it gives me to quickly progress through my studies and work to accomplish the goals I have set for myself. One of my goals is to finish college by the time I am eighteen—the same time at which most of my peers will be just beginning their pursuit of a traditional college education. Once I finish this course of accelerated learning, I anticipate using the time I would otherwise have spent in a classroom, serving others and gaining life skills.

As I progress through my studies, the degree plan has been an indispensable tool. It has given me a track on which to run and a glimpse of what awaits me. Because it provides structure for my studies, I can see how the things I am currently learning will relate to future tests and courses I will be taking. It is certainly true that "no wind is favorable for the one who knows not the port for which he is bound." I'm thankful for the sense of direction and focus that my Accelerated Distance Learning program has given me as I prepare for the future.

Earning a degree through Charter Oak will allow David to get an early start on his studies because there is no age restriction and the school allows students to complete a higher percentage of the degree through credit-by-examination. This course of study is a good foundation for a Master's program in business or science.

a. *These are typical first-year college courses that would usually take over a year to finish, but David plans on doing it in half the time.*

DAVID'S DEGREE-COMPLETION WORKSHEET			
BACHELOR OF SCIENCE WITH A CONCENTRATION IN INFORMATION SYSTEMS			
CHARTER OAK STATE COLLEGE			

SUBJECT CATEGORY	COURSE CREDIT	SUBJECT CREDIT	SECTION CREDIT
a. I. General Education Requirements			36
Aesthetic Dimensions		3	
Music Theory I – Portfolio	3		
Ethical Dimensions and Citizenship		3	
Introduction to Criminal Justice – DANTES	3		
Written Communication		6	
English Composition with Essay – CLEP	6		
Global Society		3	
International Business – Community College, Guided Study	3		

Subject Category	Course Credit	Subject Credit	Section Credit
Historical Development		3	
b. Introduction to History and Sociology – CLEP	3		
Relationship to Groups and Communities		3	
b. Introduction to Macroeconomics – CLEP	3		
Analytic and Quantitative Reasoning and Data Interpretation		3	
b. College-Level Math – CLEP	3		
Research		3	
Composition and Literature	3		
Scientific Process		6	
b. College Science – CLEP	6		
Western Civilization and Culture		3	
Contemporary Western Europe – DANTES	3		
c. II. Liberal Arts			24 - 48
d. Violin I and II – Portfolio	6		
d. Orchestra I - Portfolio	3		
Introduction to Humanities – CLEP	6		
Introduction to Microeconomics – CLEP	3		
Algebra Trigonometry – CLEP	3		
Calculus – CLEP	6		
Additional Liberal Arts Credits		21	
e. III. Concentration – Information Systems Studies			36
Introduction to Information Systems – CLEP	3		
Digital Logic	3		
Introductory Statistics – DANTES	3		
Database Management and Design	3		
Systems Analysis and Design	3		
Computer Systems Networking	3		
Computer Organization	3		
Principles of Marketing – CLEP	3		
More Concentration Electives	12		
IV. Free Electives – Additional Credit needed to equal a total of 120			
f. More Business and Computer Courses		9 - 24	
Total			120

b. David will first complete all five of the CLEP General Exams. These first 30 credits will fit into almost any degree program. Later, he will move on to earn credit through more specialized exams like Marketing, Statistics, and Introduction to Information Systems. Finally, he will work on completing portfolios and correspondence courses for the requirements in his concentration.

c. This component of a degree program is very flexible.

d. David's previous music studies and performances can be documented and included in a portfolio for credit.

e. Online courses and independent studies completed through other colleges will be transferred to Charter Oak.

f. An advisor will assist David in planning these additional requirements

There is a vast difference between a person with vision and a visionary person. The person with a vision talks little but does much. The person who is visionary talks much but does nothing. Become a student with vision, make your strategy, and pursue your goals in an organized fashion.

Twenty-One Years Old and Some College Credit: Jared Yates

Jared has always loved history, politics, and government studies and would like to work with government officials. Because he wants to save money for a master's program, make quick progress, and have the flexibility to pursue some exciting internships, Excelsior College's bachelor of arts degree with a concentration in political science seems to be tailor-made for him. Excelsior will provide Jared with a quality learning experience that will more than adequately prepare him for the challenges of graduate school.

Jared's newly acquired accelerated learning skills are really helping him. Because he took the time to apply the techniques discussed throughout this book and properly organize himself, he's been able to dramatically increase his learning speed. Before being introduced to accelerated learning, Jared doubted that he would ever complete a college degree, and yet now he anticipates going on to graduate school. Jared should be able to complete his undergraduate and master's degrees in less than four years—the same amount of time that it takes most students to simply complete their bachelor's!

STUDENT'S POINT OF VIEW: *Learning Skills, Gaining Life Experience, and Earning a Credential*
NAME: *Jared Yates*
HOME STATE: *Florida*
MAJOR: *Bachelor of Arts, Political Science*
COLLEGE: *Excelsior College*
AGE AT GRADUATION: *Currently enrolled*
CURRENT AGE: *21*

How do you acquire a recognized credential without entangling yourself in the inefficiencies and potentially harmful influences of on-campus college life? I puzzled over this question until I learned about distance learning.

My plan is to gain valuable, real-life experience through internships, obtaining both my bachelor's and master's degrees—for less time and money than most students spend to obtain just their bachelor's!

I believe that Accelerated Distance Learning will help me reach my goals much more quickly and efficiently than any other educational program I could have pursued. By doing this, I am preparing for the future in many more ways than simply completing a degree. I am able to focus my learning on skills that will be invaluable to me throughout my life.

a. JARED'S DEGREE-COMPLETION WORKSHEET BACHELOR OF SCIENCE WITH A CONCENTRATION IN INFORMATION SYSTEMS EXCELSOIR COLLEGE			
SUBJECT CATEGORY	COURSE CREDIT	SUBJECT CREDIT	SECTION CREDIT
I. General Education Requirements / Liberal Arts			90
English Composition		6	
English Composition – ECE	6		
Humanities		12	
Humanities – CLEP	6		
American Literature – CLEP	6		
Social Sciences		12	
Social Studies and History – CLEP	6		
Macro Economics – CLEP	3		
Micro Economics – CLEP	3		
Natural Sciences and Mathematics		12	
Natural Sciences – CLEP	6		
College Math – CLEP	6		
a. Liberal Arts Electives and Depth Requirement		48	
Civil War and Reconstruction – DANTES	3		
Rise and Fall of the Soviet Union – DANTES	3		
History of Nazi Germany – ECE	3		
History of the U.S. I – CLEP	3		
History of the U.S. II – CLEP	3		
b. Others	33		
c. II. Concentration			30
Core Requirements (for Political Science major)		9	
Introduction to Amer. Government	3		
Statistics – ECE	3		
Research Methods	3		
Intermediate and Upper Level Courses (for Political Science major, International Politics specialization)		18 – 21	
At least one semester course in each of the following subjects: **a.** Amer. Gov. **b.** Public Policy **c.** Comparative Politics	9+		
Three courses for concentration in International Politics: **1.** International Law **2.** Inter. Security **3.** Foreign Policy	9		
Electives – Additional Courses in Political Science			
The American Dream Part I – ECE	6		
Total			120

A look at Excelsior College's Web site and prospectus gave Jared a good idea of the kind and number of subjects that will be included in his degree.

a. This depth requirement obliges Jared to gain additional expertise in a specific subject. Because Jared is such a history buff, this was an easy choice.

b. When he begins working with an advisor, Jared will decide which courses and distance-learning methods will work best for these remaining credits.

c. The courses within the specialization will be chosen once Jared enrolls, transfers the credits he's been earning, and begins working with an advisor. These courses will be completed through independent studies, online courses, and more credit by exam.

A CPA in the Making: Erik Bonstrom

Although Erik only recently started working toward a degree in accounting, he hopes to finish within the next eight months. While most accounting majors pay over $100,000 for their education, Erik's plan will allow him to receive a top-notch education for less than $5,000.

Erik must pass the CPA exam to become a certified accountant. He has carefully checked with both the school and his state's accounting board to make sure that the program he has chosen will prepare him for the licensing exams and will be accepted by the state.

A traditional classroom would mainly focus on only theoretical aspects of accounting. Instead, Erik has spent time working in the accounting departments of two nonprofit organizations. These experiences have given

STUDENT'S POINT OF VIEW: *Reaching My Goal in One-Fourth the Time*

NAME: *Erik Bonstrom*

HOME STATE: *Iowa*

MAJOR: *Bachelor of Science in Business Administration, Accounting*

COLLEGE: *Thomas Edison College*

AGE AT GRADUATION: *Currently enrolled*

CURRENT AGE: *20*

For many years I have had the goal of becoming a "certified public accountant." At the same time, I had no interest in spending five years in college and the substantial amount of money that would be required. When I discovered Accelerated Distance Learning, I immediately recognized it as the best choice for my future. Through this new paradigm of education, I'll be able to reach my goal of becoming a CPA in one-fourth of the normal required time and for less than one-tenth of the cost! Now that I have become an accelerated learner I am able to compact a whole semester of study into only a few weeks. For example, on one Saturday I took 12 semester hours worth of tests after only studying for a week and a half! Even more incredible is the fact that the cost of those credits was less than one hundred dollars! I believe that the life experiences that I'm gaining on the job would have been lost had I been in a classroom. I'm also very confident that my education is preparing me for a successful future in accounting. Furthermore, I'm excited that I will be able to begin my career in accounting with absolutely no personal debt. The unique training that I am receiving is preparing me for my profession and equipping me to serve the needs of the business community.

Erik a better understanding of the real world of accounting and will make a great portfolio for credit.

When asked if his current course of study is too intense, he states, "In light of what I'm saving, it is certainly worth the effort!"

SUBJECT CATEGORY	COURSE CREDIT	SUBJECT CREDIT	SECTION CREDIT
ERIK'S DEGREE-COMPLETION WORKSHEET BACHELOR OF SCIENCE IN BUSINESS ADMINISTRATION—ACCOUNTING **THOMAS EDISON STATE COLLEGE**			
I. General Education Requirements / Liberal Arts			48
English Composition		6	
English Composition With Essay – CLEP	6		
Humanities		12	
Humanities – CLEP	6		
a. Biblical Psychology – Portfolio	3		
Introduction to World Religions – DANTES	3		
Social Sciences		12	
History & Social Sciences – CLEP	6		
Micro Economics – CLEP	3		
Macro Economics – CLEP	3		
Natural Sciences and Mathematics		9	
College Mathematics – CLEP	6		
Natural Sciences – CLEP	3		
General Education Electives / Liberal Arts Electives		9	
Analyzing & Interpreting Literature – CLEP	6		
Natural Sciences – CLEP	3		
II. Professional Business Requirements			60
Core Requirements		33	
Information Systems & Computer Applications – CLEP	3		
Introduction To Business Law – CLEP	3		
Introduction To Accounting – CLEP	6		
Principles of Marketing – CLEP	3		
Principles of Statistics – DANTES	3		
Introduction to Operations Management – TECEP	3		
Business Finance – TECEP	3		
Business in Society – TECEP	3		

Erik was able to get started on his degree planning worksheet by simply going to Thomas Edison's Web site and downloading the degree and specialization sheets for his major. Now that he has been able to get a feel for the kinds of courses he'll be taking, and knows approximately how much time and expense this plan will involve, he has enrolled with Thomas Edison and will begin working one-on- one with an advisor in finalizing his degree program plan.

a. Because Erik has attended numerous seminars and has real life experience in this area he plans to earn this credit through portfolio assessment.

b. *These required accounting courses will be completed through the local community college using a number of flexible methods including credit-by-examination, independent studies, and online courses.*

c. *To save time and money, Erik has targeted his portfolio assessment for the completion of upper level credits that fall within his specialization. Through his past work and volunteer Experience, Erik has a good working knowledge of accounting and will be able to make a claim for credit. In the future, these portfolios will be wonderful tools for Erik to use as part of his resume.*

Subject Category	Course Credit	Subject Credit	Section Credit
Business Policy – TECEP	3		
Principles of Management – CLEP	3		
Specialization		18	
b. Intermediate Accounting I – Community College	3		
b. Intermediate Accounting II – Community College	3		
b. Financial Accounting II – Community College	3		
c. Cost Accounting – Portfolio	3		
Managerial Accounting – TECEP	3		
Tax Accounting –TECEP	3		
Business Electives		9	
Managerial Communications – Portfolio	3		
d. Financial Institutions & Markets –TECEP	3		
d. Security Analysis & Portfolio Man -TECEP	3		
III. Free Electives			12
e. Calculus With Elementary Functions – CLEP	6		
Algebra – Trigonometry – CLEP	6		
Total			120

d. *By planning to take Thomas Edison State College Exams like these, Erik has found a fast way to get the 30 additional business credits needed to become a CPA.*

e. *These free electives can be filled with pretty much any accredited course. For a math wiz like Erik that's an easy choice.*

TIME TO GET STARTED!

Now you are ready to start designing your own degree-completion worksheet. You have already learned how to get organized and develop a focused study schedule. Because I've practiced these techniques myself, I know that they can save you thousands of dollars, years of inefficient classroom time, and many lost opportunities. What you have learned has the potential to dramatically improve your education and your future. Use these tools well, share them with others, and enjoy the benefits!

THE MOUNTAINTOP

You're getting close. Graduation Point looms in front of you, and your anticipation grows with the thought of climbing the mountain that first inspired your hiking trip. Although not a sheer cliff, Graduation Point will take effort, and you will once again put to use the equipment and climbing skills that have brought you to this point with speed and safety.

With confidence, you begin your ascent of Graduation Point. As the climb becomes steeper, you employ the hiking tips you learned from the Guide Book. You speed to the top, your anticipation giving you new strength for the last part of your journey.

Cresting the peak, you are filled with emotion as you realize you have reached your goal—you made it to the top! You have conquered.

Your eyes scan the vast horizon which this vantage point yields. With many other mountain ranges in view, the possibilities for future challenges are endless. Graduation Point won't be my only accomplishment, you think as you consider the adventures ahead. This is only the beginning!

Congratulations! You've come a long way. It's time to review the ground you've covered and examine how your journey thus far has prepared you for an exciting future.

Graduation Point:

Your Degree and Beyond

You have just completed what I hope will be a life-changing book. You no longer have a reason to spend four long years sitting in a classroom, spending huge amounts of money, subjecting yourself to the mercy of your school and professors, and starting your work without any real experience or clear direction. There is a better way, and you have discovered it.

"So teach us to number our days, that we may apply our hearts unto wisdom." —The Bible, Proverbs 90:12

We've covered a lot of information in this book, including:

- Why Accelerated Distance Learning is a better choice than traditional college.

- How and when to use credit-by-examination, portfolio assessment, online courses, and guided studies.

- How to remember, read, and write information quickly and effectively.

- How to decide in which college to enroll, credit-earning options, and how you'll pay for it all!

- How to increase efficiency by organizing your time and your environment.

Additionally, you have learned how to take these new methods and techniques and incorporate them into a strategy that will allow you to earn your degree in a fraction of the time. Take the principles you have learned from this book, apply them, and refer back to them often as you make progress toward earning your degree.

While the focus of this book has been primarily on how to earn your college degree through Accelerated Distance Learning, the book also outlines a method for preparing for the challenges and opportunities of the twenty-first century. Those who follow the strategy outlined within

Principle #5: LIFELONG
LEARNING. The
amount of informa-
tion in man's store of
knowledge is exploding
at an
increasing rate of
growth—you must
keep up.

Principle #9:
INFLUENCE. One life
can make an impact
in the world.

"The most tremendous
experience in life is
the learning process."
—Charley "T" Jones

this book will, in the end, be prepared for the great opportunities of this age, as our society transitions into a knowledge-based economy.

A knowledge-based economy requires knowledge workers. Knowledge workers understand how to deal with vast amounts of new information and are able to keep up within a climate of constant change by continually upgrading their skills through flexible online learning programs. Knowledge workers know how to stay on top of the game through lifelong learning. The learning skills required of the knowledge worker are the very skills that every accelerated distance learner will already possess.

It's no longer enough to go to school for four years, earn a degree, and enter the job market. Today there is no single "Graduation Point." Lifelong learning is an essential quality that every knowledge worker will need if they hope to successfully operate in the knowledge economy. There will be many more "mountains" in life for you to climb in the future, and your first climb toward receiving a college credential will have prepared you for what lies ahead.

I hope that by now you've sensed my excitement about this new paradigm of college education. You have the opportunity to be a "pioneer" on the new "trail" of Accelerated Distance Learning. The trail is fairly well-established, but most people are still using the old, slow, expensive way. I urge you to share the concepts of this book with others so they, too, can experience the exciting benefits of the "new trail." You can potentially save them thousands of hard-earned dollars and countless hours of precious time, simply by suggesting that they purchase their own copy of this book.

It has been a pleasure for me to accompany you this far. I'm glad that our journey together doesn't stop here. I know you want to move toward your destination as quickly as possible, and I want to help you do it. If you purchased this book directly from me, then you should be hearing from me regularly with more great suggestions on how we can work together. If you didn't buy this book directly from me, I hope you'll take the initiative to get in touch. Please do it! There are many other effective tools designed to assist you along the way, and we are continually discovering and developing some of the best.

You have an exciting adventure ahead of you. Nothing would please me more than to hear the story of your triumphs along the way. My goal is to continue encouraging others with the success stories of other accelerated distance learners. I am also eager to hear your tips and new discoveries that will help make future editions of this book even better.

I wish you the very best and look forward to hearing from you soon!

About the Author

During the past several years, Brad Voeller has spent time at home and abroad researching distance and accelerated learning methods. Formerly a teacher in Shandong, China, he has had a growing desire to facilitate the spread of distance and accelerated learning methods worldwide.

In 2000, Brad founded the Global Leadership Institute, Inc., and its subsidiary, Global Learning Strategies. Through this work, he hopes to encourage and train a host of young people who will use distance and accelerated learning methods to become the next generation of global leaders and entrepreneurs. A writer, speaker, and educational consultant, he seeks to present the most helpful, up-to-date, and effective methods for Accelerated Distance Learning.

In the future, Brad plans on assisting developing countries that may benefit from utilizing distance-learning technology for their educational needs.

You can reach him at the following address:

20475 Hwy 46 W
Ste. 180 #162
Spring Branch, TX 78070
(bradv@GlobalLearningStrategies.org

Appendix A:
Glossary of Distance-Learning Terms

A

Academic advisor. College faculty member who works with students to plan courses of study to meet their degree requirements.

Academic ESL/EFL (English as a Second/Foreign Language). Prepares students whose first language is not English for college study in the United States.

Academic year. One year's worth of study at a college, usually two or three semesters and occurring within a one-year period.

Accreditation. Recognition that an institution meets a set of educational standards. Not all accreditation is equal.

Accrediting agency. A private organization that establishes a set of standards and verifies whether educational institutions meet those standards.

Adjunct faculty. Part-time faculty member, often teaches at multiple institutions.

Admissions. Department within a college that handles student enrollment.

Admissions Specialists. These college staff members are usually a good resource when trying to gather information about the distance-learning options available through a certain college. They can tell you what to do to get started.

Advanced Placement. Exams offered through high schools in cooperation with the College Board. Generally, a score of three or higher will qualify for college credit at participating colleges.

Advising office. Department within a college that answers student's questions. May offer an "advising hotline" that provides students with instant access to needed information.

Alma mater. The school from which you graduate.

Alumni. A school's graduates.

American College Testing (ACT). An organization that administers standardized college admissions tests given to students at the high school level.

American Council on Education (ACE). Private organization that evaluates academic equivalencies for corporate and military training.

Articulated credit. Credit acquired through some form of portfolio analysis. See *Portfolio Analysis*.

Associate's degree. Degree usually awarded after completion of 60 credits and traditionally earned in two years.

B

Bachelor's degree. Degree usually awarded after completion of 120 credits and traditionally earned in four years.

Bursar. College department or official that handles tuition and payments.

C

Campus. The main facility of a college. Might include grounds, buildings, dormitories, etc. The campus of a nontraditional college might consist solely of offices.

Center for Independent Learning. Found in some colleges that encourage distance learning, this division offers alternatives such as online courses, telecourses, and independent studies.

Certificate. Credential awarded upon completion of a study program that doesn't result in a degree, but is focused on a specific topic or course.

Certificate program. Study program designed for students who aren't pursuing a formal degree, but wish to complete an academic course or program.

Certification. Professional credential awarded for passing a competency examination in a field of employment. Some colleges award credit for professional certifications.

CLEP (College-Level Examination Program). National program sponsored by the College Board through which students may receive college credit by taking tests for knowledge that was acquired independently.

College. Institutions offering programs leading to the Associate's, Bachelor's, and sometimes higher degrees. While often used interchangeably with university, traditionally a university consists of several colleges.

College Board, The. Nonprofit membership organization that provides tests and other educational services for students, schools, and colleges. The membership is composed of more than 2,700 colleges and universities.

Community college. A two-year school, offering programs leading to an Associate's degree. Sometimes reffered to as a junior college.

Correspondence course. A course offered by mail and completed through home study. Usually requires one or two examinations and completion of writing assignments.

Course description. Explanation of the major points taught in a course, usually found in a college catalog or college web site. An essential tool in the portfolio assessment process.

Credit. Unit used to measure completion of college courses. College courses are usually 1–6 credits. Each credit represents the number of hours spent in class each week. A one-credit course would commonly be a class that met one hour each week for one semester.

Credit-by-examination. A method used by distance learners to receive college credit for what they already know. A passing test score results in college credit.

Curriculum. Set of courses that must be

completed in order to meet the requirements of a degree program.

D

DANTES (Defense Activity for Nontraditional Educational Support). Credit-by-examination program developed by the military, open to anyone and widely accepted by colleges.

Department of Education. The U.S. government agency that works in conjunction with the various state Departments of Education.

Diploma. Certificate awarded for the completion of a degree program.

Distance Education and Training Council (DETC). U.S. agency that accredits distance-learning programs.

Distance learning. System of education in which the student and instructor are remote from each other.

Doctorate. Advanced degree granted for postgraduate university study. Doctorates include Ph.D, Ed.D, J.D., and M.D.

E

EFC–Expected Family Contribution. A calculation used to determine your share of the total college tuition costs. This calculation is based on an analysis of your family's income and assets and will be a determining factor for many grants and scholarships.

Elective. Course that isn't required but may be taken to earn credits toward the total number required for a degree.

External. Remote from a school's main campus. External degrees may be earned through home study or at a school's satellite location.

F

Financial aid. Grants, scholarships, student loans, and tax incentives that are made available to students. Generally distance-learning students also qualify for financial aid.

G

Grade Point Average. Usually an average of all grades a student earns.

Grants. Financial aid distributed to students by federal and state governments that does not require repayment.

Graduate Record Examination (GRE). Standardized test of math and verbal aptitude required by many institutions for admission to a graduate program. Some schools offer undergraduate credit for successfully passing GRE subject exams.

Graduate study. College-level courses for students who have already obtained an undergraduate degree.

Guided study. Distance learning method that involves working with a professor one-on-one to complete a college course.

I

Independent study. Same as guided study. See *Guided Study.*

Interlibrary loan. Wonderful library service that makes buying textbooks unnecessary. Even the smallest local library can be used to obtain a wealth of resources from other libraries around the world.

Internship. Job designed to help you learn practical skills through real-life workplace responsibilities.

J

Junior/Community college. Two-year institution, usually state funded, that offers inexpensive college-level courses and grants associate degrees.

L

Learning contract. Agreement between a learning institution and student specifying a customized study program a student will follow and what credits or degrees will be awarded when it is successfully completed.

Liberal Arts. Institution or degree program that provides a broad education in traditional topics such as literature, art, mathematics, and science.

Lifelong learning. The process of continually keeping your knowledge up-to-date—made much easier by distance learning.

Lower-level/Upper-level credit. 100 or 200 level courses are considered lower level; 300 or 400 level courses are considered upper level.

M

Major. Main focus of study in a degree-granting program at the university level.

Mentor. Individual who serves as a model and teacher for a work or educational experience.

Minor. Focus of university study secondary to a major.

N

Narrative. Portfolio document that explains the nature of a learning experience and the knowledge that was acquired through that experience.

Noncredit. Course taken without formal credit being awarded. Noncredit courses are often zero-level remedial courses.

Nonresident. Student enrolled at a state university outside of the state where he or she officially resides. Tuition is usually much higher for nonresidents.

P

Pass/Fail. Grading system that gives no specific letter or number grade—students either pass or fail. Pass/fail courses result in credit but are usually not computed into a GPA calculation.

Portfolio. The actual document produced in the portfolio assessment process and submitted with a claim for college credit.

Portfolio assessment. A method for students to receive college credit for knowledge gained in prior education, work experience, on-the-job training, extensive reading, military training, and other learning experiences. Also referred to as "credit by demonstrated competence" or "articulated credit."

Portfolio assessment advisors. Specialized advisors with expertise in portfolio assessment who are able to provide students with key information that will help them complete the portfolio process.

Portfolio study. A method for students with partial knowledge of a subject to gain credit by both documenting past learning experiences and doing additional studies where needed.

Practicum. Component of a curriculum that requires you to practically apply classroom learning.

Prerequisite. A listed course or other requirement that must be completed before enrolling in a course.

Proctored exam. Exam that requires the student taking it be monitored. Some distance-learning programs require students to have exams proctored at a local test center.

Q

Quarter and Semester hours. Most colleges grant credits in semester hours, but some grant credits in quarter hours. If you are planning to transfer credit from one school to another, you will have to figure out course equivalencies. A quarter hour is equal to two-thirds semester hour. Divide quarter hours by 1½ to convert to semester hours. Multiply semester hours by 1½ to convert to quarter hours.

1.5 quarter hours = 1 semester hour
3.0 quarter hours = 2 semester hours
4.5 quarter hours = 3 semester hours

6.0 quarter hours = 4 semester hours
7.5 quarter hours = 5 semester hours

R

Regional Accrediting Agency. There are six major accrediting agencies in the United States that sets standards and coordinates those standards among other agencies to ensure consistency in academic standards.

Registrar. Department in a university that handles enrollment and course registration; may also be used to refer to the person in charge of that department.

Registration. The act of enrolling in a course and paying any tuition due.

S

Scholarships. Financial aid given away by schools, other institutions, and individuals that doesn't require repayment. Might be given for special talents or special needs.

Scholastic Aptitude Test (SAT). Standardized test for college admissions typically given to high school students; designed by the College Board.

Semester. Period of time (usually 16 weeks) during which college students take and complete courses. Most institutions have two semesters a year and sometimes a third semester in the summer.

Syllabus. Outline of all the lectures, exams, and assignments that make up a course, usually containing a list of resources used for the course.

T

Traditional colleges. Places that make learning boring and ineffective by limiting a student's opportunities to practically apply learning.

Transcript. Official record of a student's educational courses, credits, and grades.

Transfer credit. Credit that is moved from one institution to another.

U

Undergraduate. Study at the bachelor's degree level; may also be used to refer to a student studying at this level.

Z

Zero-level courses. Courses with numbers lower than 100 are noncredit courses and do not apply to degree programs. They are usually offered for developmental or continuing education.

Appendix B:
Credit-by-Examination Programs

Graduate Record Examination (GRE)
Biochemistry, Cell, and Molecular Biology
Biology (0-24)
Chemistry (0-24)
Computer Science (0-24)
English Literature (0-24)
Mathematics (0-24)
Physics (0-24)
Psychology (0-24)

New York State University Foreign
Language Exams
American
Chinese-Cantonese
Chinese-Mandarin
French
German
Greek (Modern)
Hebrew
Italian
Japanese
Korean
Russian
Spanish

For a complete listing of all 50+ language exams, visit www.scps.nyu.edu

EXCELSIOR COLLEGE EXAMINATIONS (ECE)
Arts and Science:
Abnormal Psychology (3)
American Dream (6)
Anatomy and Physiology (6)
College Writing (3)
Cultural Diversity (3)
English Composition (6)
Ethics: Theory and Practice (3)
Foundations of Gerontology (3)
Juvenile Delinquency (3)
Life Span Development Psychology (3)
Microbiology (3)
Pathophysiology (3)
Psychology of Adulthood and Aging (3)
Religions of the World (3)
Research Methods in Psychology (3)
Social Psychology (3)
Statistics (3)
World Conflicts (3)
World Population (3)

Business:
Human Resource Management (3)
Labor Relations (3)
Organizational Behavior (3)

Education:
Reading Instruction in the Elementary
School (6)

Nursing:
Fundamentals in Nursing (8)
Maternal/Child Nursing (AS) (6)
Maternity Nursing (3)
Nursing Concepts 1
Nursing Concepts 2
Nursing Concepts 3
Nursing Concepts 4
Nursing Concepts 5
Nursing Concepts 6

CLEP
General:
College Mathematics (6)
English Composition (6)
Humanities (6)

Natural Sciences (6)

Social Sciences and History (6)

Business:

Introductory Accounting (6)

Introductory Business Law (3)

Information Systems and Computer Applications (3)

Principles of Management (3)

Principles of Marketing (3)

Science and Mathematics:

Calculus With Elementary Functions (6)

College Algebra (3)

College Algebra–Trigonometry (3)

General Biology (6)

General Chemistry (6)

Pre-Calculus (3)

History and Social Sciences:

American Government (3)

Human Growth and Development (3)

History of the United States I: Early Colonization to 1877 (3)

History of the United States II: 1865 to the Present (3)

Introduction to Educational Psychology (3)

Introductory Psychology (3)

Introductory Sociology (3)

Principles of Macroeconomics (3)

Principles of Microeconomics (3)

Western Civilization I: Ancient Near East to 1648 (3)

Western Civilization II: 1648 to the Present (3)

Composition and Literature:

American Literature (6)

Analyzing and Interpreting Literature (6)

English Literature (6)

Freshman College Composition (6)

Foreign Languages:

College French–
Level 1 (6)
Level 2 (12)

College German–
Level 1 (6)

Level 2 (12)

College Spanish–
Level 1 (6)
Level 2 (12)

TECEP

English Composition:

English Composition I (3)

English Composition II (3)

Humanities:

Art History I (3)

Art History II (3)

Introduction to News Reporting (3)

Introduction to the Art of Theater (3)

Introduction to the History of Film (3)

Public Relations Thought and Practice (3)

Shakespeare I (3)

Technical Writing (3)

Social Science:

Alcohol Abuse: Fundamental Facts (3)

Behavior Modification Techniques in Col-Counseling (3)

Developmental Psychology (3)

Industrial Psychology (3)

Introduction to Counseling (3)

Introduction to Political Science (3)

Introduction to Social Psychology (3)

Introduction to Transactional Analysis (3)

Labor Relations & Collective Bargaining (3)

Advanced Labor Relations & Collective Bargaining (3)

Marriage and the Family (3)

Organizational Behavior (3)

Psychology of Personality (3)

Psychology of Women (3)

Research in Experimental Psychology (3)

Social Gerontology (3)

Substance Abuse: Fundamental Facts (3)

Thanatology: An Understanding of Death and Dying (3)

Natural Science/Mathematics:

Anatomy and Physiology (6)

BASIC (3)
Physics I (3)
Physics II (3)
Operating Systems (3)
Physical Geology (3)
Principles of Statistics (3)
QBASIC (3)
The Science of Nutrition (3)
C Programming (3)

Business:

Advanced Labor Relations and Collective
Advertising (3)
Business Law (3)
Business in Society (3)
Business Policy (3)
Database Management (3)
Financial Institutions and Markets (3)
Human Resources Management (3)
International Finance and Trade (3)
Introduction to Computer Information
Systems (3)
Introduction to Marketing (3)
Introduction to Operations Management (3)
Labor Relations and Collective Bargaining (3)
Marketing Channels (3)
Marketing Communications (3)
Marketing Management Strategy (3)
Marketing Research (3)
Organizational Behavior (3)
Principles of Management (3)
Principles of Finance (3)
Sales Management (3)
Security Analysis & Portfolio Management (3)

Human Services:

Community Health (3)
Counselor Training: Short-Term Client
Systems (3)
Introduction to Human Services (3)
Kinesiology (3)

Free Electives:

Word Processing Fundamentals (3)

OHIO UNIVERSITY EXAMS (Qtr.Hrs)

African American Studies (AAS)

101 African American History I, 1526-1865 (4)

225 History of the Black Worker (4)

Aviation (AVN)

110 Basic Aeronautics (4)
340 Cross-Country Flight (4)
350 Instrument System Regulations & Procedures (4)
405 Advanced Cross-Countries (4)
435 Flight Engineer (4)
450 Instrument Instructor Ground
Instruction (3)
460 ATP Ground Instruction (4)
240 Private Pilot Flight Course (4)

Biological Sciences (BIOS)

103 Human Biology (5)
345 Human Physiology (4)
384 Bioethics: Bioethical Problems in Biology and Medicine (5)
390H Biology and the Future of Man (5)

Business Law (BUSL)

255 Law and Society (4)
356 Law of the Management Process (4)
357 Law of Commercial Transactions (4)
360 Law of Health Care (4)
442 Law of Property and Real Estate (4)

Business Management Technology (BMT)

110 Introduction to Management (4)
140 Concepts of Marketing (4)
150 Elements of Supervision (4)
170 Small Business Operations (4)
189 Independent Study: Personal
Financial Planning (4)
200 Introduction to Business Computing (4)
210 Managing Finance in Business (4)
220 Concepts of Purchasing Management (4)
260 Business Report Writing (4)
270 Advertising Concepts (4)
275 Managerial Planning (4)
280 Concepts of Labor and Management
Relations (4)
285 Government and Business (4)

288 Computer Applications for Management (4)

289 Special Topics: Fundamentals of Investing (4)

Classics and World Religions (CLWR)

311 Islam (4)

321 Hinduism (4)

341 and Taoism (5)

Communications Studies (COMS)

101 Fundamentals of Human Communication (4)

103 Fundamentals of Public Speaking (4)

Deaf Studies and Interpreting

111 Sign Language and Deaf Culture I (4)

112 Sign Language and Deaf Culture II (4)

Economics (ECON)

103 Principles of Microeconomics (4)

104 Principles of Macroeconomics (4)

303 Microeconomics (4)

304 Macroeconomics (4)

320 Labor Economics (4)

340 International Trade (4)

360 Money and Banking (4)

Education (EDCE)

203 Credit for Experience: Portfolio Development (4)

Electronic Technology (ETCH)

110 Basic Electronics (4)

112 Industrial Electronics (4)

120 Digital Electronics (4)

134 Direct Current Circuit Analysis (5)

135 Alternating Current Circuit Analysis (5)

220 Electrical Motors, Control Circuits, and Computers (4)

236A Microprocessor & Comp. Basics (4)

236B Microprocessor & Comp. Basics (4)

289 Electronic Trouble-Shooting & Repair (4)

English (ENG)

150 Developmental Writing Skills (4)

151 Writing in Rhetoric I (5)

152 Writing and Reading (5)

153 Writing and Reading: Gender (5)

200 Introduction to Literature (4)

201 Critical Approaches to Fiction (4)

202 Critical Approaches to Poetry (4)

203 Critical Approaches to Drama (4)

301 Shakespeare: The Histories (4)

302 Shakespeare: The Comedies (4)

303 Shakespeare: The Tragedies (4)

305J Technical Writing (4)

307J Writing and Research in English Studies (4)

308J Writing and Rhetoric II (4)

312 English Literature: 1500-1660 (4)

313 English Literature: 1660-1800 (4)

321 American Literature to 1865 (4)

322 American Literature: 1865 to 1918 (4)

323 American Literature: 1918 to Present (4)

325 Women and Literature (4)

361 Creative Writing: Fiction (4)

362 Creative Writing: Poetry (4)

Humanities (HUM)

107 Humanities—Great Books (4)

108 Humanities—Great Books (4)

109 Humanities—Great Books: Modern (4)

307 Humanities—Great Books (4)

308 Humanities—Great Books (4)

309 Humanities—Great Books: Modern (4)

Finance (FIN)

325 Foundations of Finance (4)

Foreign Languages and Literatures

111 Elementary French (4)

112 Elementary French (4)

113 Elementary French (4)

211 Intermediate French (4)

212 Intermediate French (4)

213 Intermediate French (4)

111 Elementary German (4)

112 Elementary German (4)

113 Elementary German (4)

211 Intermediate German (4)

212 Intermediate German (4)

213 Intermediate German (4)

111 Elementary Spanish (4)

112 Elementary Spanish (4)

113 Elementary Spanish (4)

211 Intermediate Spanish (4)
212 Intermediate Spanish (4)
213 Intermediate Spanish (4)
Geography (GEOG)
121 Human Geography (4)
Health Sciences (HLTH)
217 Intro to Health Care Organizations (4)

Health Sciences-Industrial Hygiene (HI)
200 Introduction to Industrial Hygiene and Occupational Safety and Health (4)
History (HIST)
101 Western Civilization in Modern Times (4)
102 Western Civilization in Modern Times (4)
103 Western Civilization in Modern Times (4)
133 Intro to Non-Western History Since 1750: Cross-Cultural Perspectives (4)
246 The Rise of Modern Asia (4)
303 The United States in World War II (4)
317A Ohio History to 1851 (4)
317B Ohio History Since 1851 (4)
329A Ancient Egypt and Mesopotamia (4)
329B Ancient Greece (4)
329C Ancient Rome (4)
375 World War I (4)

Health and Consumer Sciences
HCCF 160 Intro to Child Development (4)
HCFN 128 Intro to Nutrition (4)
HCRM 250 The Consumer in American Society (4)

International Lit: Modern Languages
336 Spanish Literature in English (4)
336B Spanish Literature in English (4)

Journalism (JOUR)
311 History of American Journalism (4)
411 Communication Law (3)

Law Enforcement Technology (LET)
100 Intro to Law Enforement Technology (3)
120 Constitutional, Criminal, and Civil Law (3)
130 Interviewing and Report Writing (3)
260 Criminal Investigation (3)

275 Law Enforcement and the Deaf (4)
Marketing (MKT)
202 Marketing Principles (4)
450 Management of Promotion (4)
Mathematics (MATH)
101 Basic Mathematics (4)
109 Consumer Mathematics (4)
113 Algebra (5)
115 Pre-Calculus (5)
163A Introduction to Calculus I (4)
163B Introduction to Calculus II (3)
211 Elementary Linear Algebra (4)
250 Intro to Probability and Statistics I (4)
263A Calculus I (4)
263B Calculus II (4)
263C Calculus III (4)
263D Calculus IV (4)
340 Differential Equations (4)
Medical Terminology (MAT)
140 Medical Terminology for the Medical Assistant (3)
Music (MUS)
160 Music Fundamentals (3)
321 History and Literature of Music I (3)
322 History and Literature of Music II (3)
Office Technology (OTEC)
121 Keyboarding I (4)
122 Keyboarding II (4)
130 Business Communication I (4)
231 Business Calculations (4)
Philosophy (PHIL)
101 Fundamentals of Philosophy (4)
120 Principles of Reasoning (4)
130 Intro to Ethics (4)
232 Philosophy of Art (4)
301 Introduction to Philosophy (3)
350 Philosophy of Culture (5)
Physical Educ. & Sport Sciences (PESS)
204 History & Principles of Physical Education(4)
225 History of the Sport Industry (4)
406 Organization and Administration of

Physical Education (4)

Physical Science (PSC)

100 Survey of Astronomy (4)
101 Physical World (4)
105 Color, Light, and Sound (4)
111 The Metric System (1)

Physics (PHYS)

201 Introduction to Physics (4)
202 Introduction to Physics (4)
203 Introduction to Physics (4)
251 General Physics (4)
252 General Physics (4)
253 General Physics (4)

Political Science (POL)

101 American National Government (4)

Professional Communication (PRCM)

325J Professional Communication (4)

Psychology (PSY)

101 General Psychology (5)
221 Statistics for the Behavioral Sciences (5)
275 Educational Psychology (4)
315 Behavior Genetics & Individual Differences (5)
332 Abnormal Psychology (4)
336 Social Psychology
337 Social Psychology of Justice (4)
374 Psychology of Adulthood and Aging (4)
376 Psychological Disorders of Childhood (4)
380 Psychology of Health and illness (4)

Quantitative Business Analysis (QBA)

201 Introduction to Business Statistics (4)

Sociology (SOC)

101 Introduction to Sociology (4)
260 Criminal Justice (4)
351 Elementary Research Techniques (4)
362 Criminology (4)
363 Juvenile Delinquency (4)

Theater (THAR)

270 Theater History I (4)
271 Theater History II (4)
272 Theater History III (4)

DANTES Subject Standardized Tests (DSSTs)

BUSINESS SCIENCES

Introduction to Business
Business Law II
Introduction to Computing
Principles of Finance
Principles of Financial Accounting
Management Information Systems
Money and Banking
Organizational Behavior
Personal Finance
Human Resource Management
Principles of Supervision

Humanities

Art of the Western World
An Introduction to the Modern Middle East
Introduction to World Religions
Ethics in America

Mathematics

Business Mathematics
Fundamentals of College Algebra
Principles of Statistics Astronomy
Environment & Humanity: The Race to Save the Planet Earth
Principles of Physical Geology
Principles of Physical Science I

Social Sciences

General Anthropology
Civil War and Reconstruction
Contemporary Western Europe 1946-1990
Fundamentals of Counseling
Drug & Alcohol Abuse
Human/Cultural Geography
Here's to Your Health
A History of the Vietnam War
Lifespan Developmental Psychology
Principles of Public Speaking
Technical Writing
Rise & Fall of the Soviet Union
Criminal Justice
Introduction to Law Enforcement

Education

Foundations of Education

Appendix C:

Degrees and Courses Available Online and Through Correspondence Study

The following list of degrees and courses is only a partial listing of the many courses and degrees available online and through correspondence study. Scan the list quickly and you'll see that almost anything can be studied through distance learning. With new additions being made almost weekly, this list is growing fast.

A

Accident investigation
Accounting
Administrative secretary
Advertising
Air conditioning
Air force career specialties
Airline/travel career training
Air warfare
Allied health
Animal care specialist
Appliance servicing
Army career specialties
Art composition and fundamentals
Artificial intelligence
Audio electronics
Auto detailing
Automation
Automotive electronics
Automotive mechanics
Automotive repair technician
Automotive technology

B

Banking and finance
Bartending
Beauty salon management
Bible studies

Biology
Blind, courses for
Blueprint reading
Boat design
Bookkeeping
Braille
Breastfeeding counselor
Bridal consulting
Broadcast engineering
Broadcasting radio and TV
Business administration
Business management
Business studies
Business writing

C

Career planning
Carpentry
Car rental
Cartooning
Catering
Chemistry
Child care
Children's literature
Civics
Civil engineering technology
Clerical
Coast guard career specialist

College-level subjects
College preparation
Colored stones
Color theory
Color TV technology
Commercial driver's license preparation
Commercial real estate finance
Communications
Communications technology
Computer applications
Computerized secretary
Computer literacy
Computer maintenance and repair
Computer networks
Computer programming
Computer repair technician
Computer support specialist
Computer technology
Conservation
Contracting
Cooking gourmet
Cost accounting
Counter sketching
Court reporting
Criminal justice
Cruise lines

D ───────────────
Day care management
Deaf-blind home teaching preschool children
Deaf home teaching preschool children
Dental assisting
Dental office assisting/receptionist
Design in art
Desktop publishing
Diamontology
Digital electronics
Doll repair
Drafting

Drafting with AutoCAD
Drawing
Dressmaking
Drywall installation and finishing

E ───────────────
Early childhood education
Economics
Education
EKG technology
Electrical engineering technology
Electrician
Electricity
Electroencephalographic technology
Electronics
Elementary school courses
Engineering
Engineering design
Engines and engine tune-up
English
Enterprise development
Estate management

F ───────────────
Fashion, introduction to
Fashion merchandising
FCC general radiotelephone
FCC license preparation
Finance
Financial management
Financial planning
Firearms
Fish and wildlife management
Fitness and nutrition
Floral design
Flower arrangement and floristry
Food preparation
Food service administration
Foreign policy

Forensic science
Forestry
Freelance writing
French
Front-line management
Furniture/cabinetmaking

G

Gardening
GED preparation
Gem identification
Gemology
Genealogy
Geography
Gold and precious metals
Gun repair/gunsmithing

H

Health
Health care
Health care accreditation
Health care management
Health science
Heating and air conditioning
High school subjects
History
Home-based travel agents
Home health aide
Home inspection
Home living
Home remodeling and repair
Hospitality career management
Hotel/motel career training
Hotel operations
Human relations
Human resource management
Hypnotherapy

I

Illustration
Income tax
Industrial electronics
Industrial engineering technology
Infants and toddlers with special needs
Information technology
Instrumentation
Insurance replacement appraisal
Intelligence studies
Interior decorating
Internal combustion engines
Internet Web page design
Introductory metrics
Investigation, criminal
Investigator

J

Java programming
Jewelry design and retailing
Jewelry display
Jewelry repair
Jewelry sales
Journalism
Junior high school subjects
Juris doctorate

K

Kindergarten

L

Lactation consultant
Landscaping
Landscaping design
Land warfare
Language, biblical
Language, foreign
Latin
Law, business

Law, enforcement
Law, hotel and motel
Law, medical staff
Lawyer's assistant
Leisure and corporate agency training
Legal assistant
Legal nurse consulting
Legal secretary
Legal transcriptionist
Life management
Literature
Locksmithing

M

Management
Management, small business
Marine corps career specialties
Marine craft technology
Marketing
Marketing, hotel and motel
Masonry
Mathematics
Mechanics, automotive
Mechanics, diesel
Mechanics, motorcycle
Medical assisting
Medical billing
Medical coding
Medical ethics
Medical insurance clerk
Medical office assisting/receptionist
Medical office computer specialist
Medical records technology
Medical staff law
Medical staff office administration
Medical staff organization
Medical terminology
Medical transcription
Meeting planning

Merchandizing
Microcomputer repair and services
Microcomputers
Microprocessors
Military history
Military science
Military skills
Military studies
Missions
Modeling
Mortgage banking
Motel operations
Motorcycle repair
Motor truck sales
Motor tune-up
Multimedia
Music
Music appreciation

N

Naval warfare
Networking
Nutrition

O

Occupational therapy aide
Oceanography
Oil painting

P

Paralegal
Pastoral ministries
PC repair
Pearl and bead stringing
Pearls
Personnel Management
Pet grooming
Pet shop assistant
Pharmacy technician

Philosophy

Photography

Physical fitness

Physical therapy

Physical therapy aide

Plumbing

Political science

Prehospital medicine

Preschool

Private investigation

Professional military education

Project management

Property management

Psychology

Public administration

Public management

Q

Quality management

R

Radar

Radio

Refrigeration

Real estate and finance

Real estate appraisal

Religion

Residential lending

Respiratory therapy

Restaurant management

Retailing

Robotics

S

Salesmanship

Science

Scoping

Secretarial

Sewing

Sheet metal

Short hand

Small engine repair

Social studies

Sociology

Soldering

Sound technician

Spanish

Spanish courses written in Spanish language

Special needs for infants and toddlers

Spirituality

Stenotype machine shorthand

Supervisory development

Surveying

T

Tax procedures

Teacher's aide

Telecommunications

Television

Theology

Tourism

Training and development

Transpersonal studies

Travel agency training

Travel career training

Travel counseling

Truck driving

Truck maintenance and repair

Truck selection training

Typing

U

Unconventional warfare

Unix

U.S. History

V ————————————

VCR repair
Ventilation
Vocational electives

W ————————————

Wildlife management
World history
Writing

Y ————————————

Yacht design

Z ————————————

Zoology

Appendix D:
Degree-Planning Worksheets

Degree-Completion Worksheet

Explanation: This worksheet allows you to fill in each course and course completion method and identify how you might choose to complete each of the requirements within your degree. In addition to helping you identify possibilities for your degree, this worksheet can serve as an initial plan for you to send to your advisor for evaluation.

DEGREE-COMPLETION WORKSHEET			
YOUR NAME:			
SOCIAL SECURITY NUMBER:			
DEGREE PROGRAM:			
SUBJECT CATEGORY	COURSE CREDIT	SUBJECT CREDIT	SECTION CREDIT
I. General Education Requirements/Liberal Arts			36 – 48
English Composition		3 – 6	
Humanities		6 – 9	
Social Sciences and History		6 – 12	
Natural Sciences and Mathematics		9 – 18	

Subject Category	Course Credit	Subject Credit	Section Credit
General Education Electives/Liberal Arts Electives		3 – 9	
II. Concentration			33 – 60
Core Requirements		21 – 33	
Individualized Specialization		18 – 33	
III. Free Electives			18 – 27
Total			120

Portfolio Possibility Worksheet

Explanation: This worksheet will help you brainstorm about possible subject areas for which you could claim credit through portfolio assessment.

Instructions:

My Knowledge and Experience: *List experiences and knowledge that you have acquired.*
Corresponding Academic Subject: *Identify possible subjects that would correspond.*
Evidence of My Knowledge: *List items that you could present as proof of your learning.*
Areas Needing More Study: *List aspects of the subject where your knowledge is still insufficient.*
Learning Opportunities: *List opportunities you have to strengthen your knowledge through further life experience or individual study.*

PORTFOLIO POSSIBILITY WORKSHEET				
My Knowledge and Experience	Corresponding Academic Subject	Evidence of My Knowledge	Areas Needing More Study	Learning Opportunities

Portfolio Writing Worksheet

Explanation: Use this Portfolio Writing Worksheet to help you plan how you will write your portfolio. Identify a subject that you think you can claim credit for, make sure it fits into your degree program, and you are ready to begin this worksheet.

Instructions

Course Title: *List the title of the course for which you are planning to write a portfolio.*

Course Description: *Divide the course description into distinct parts and list separately.*

My Corresponding Knowledge: *For each part of the course description, list the corresponding experience and knowledge that you have acquired.*

Supporting Evidence for Each Claim: *List one or more items of evidence that support your claim of having this knowledge.*

PORTFOLIO WRITING WORKSHEET			
Course Title	Course Description	My Corresponding Knowledge	Supporting Evidence for Each Claim

Appendix E:
Internet Resources

Distance Learning Courses:

www.lifelonglearning.com
LifeLongLearning.com
Distance-learning courses and student
resources such as financing for distance
learning

www.utexas.edu/world/lecture
The World Lecture Hall
Listings of international distance-learning
providers as well as an exhaustive listing
of links to pages created by faculty using
distance learning worldwide

Distance Learning International:

www-icdl.open.ac.uk/icdl/
International Center for Distance Learning
Online database of resources in distance
learning around the world, including
courses, teaching organizations, journal
articles, and conferences

www.cade-aced.ca
**Canadian Association of Distance
Education (CADE)**
Find out which Canadian schools are
involved in distance learning

www.baol.co.uk
**British Association for Open
Learning Ltd.**

www.icde.org
**European Council for Distance
Education**

www.studyabroad.com
For students who want to **study abroad**

Distance Learning Providers:

www.mindedge.com
The Internet University
Indexing service that lists articles, courses,
and study; more than 2,440 courses listed

www.aacc.nche.edu/allaboutcc/
snapshot.htm
**American Association of Community
Colleges**
Find information about community col-
leges in your area

Distance Learning Research:

dir.yahoo.com/Education/
        Higher_Education/
        Colleges_and_Universities/
        United_States

Yahoo Search
Helpful indices contain e-mail addresses for colleges, college departments, and student clubs

www.detc.org
The Distance Education and Training Council (DETC)
Informational resources on technology-based learning for both students and teachers

www.uwex.edu
The Distance Education Clearinghouse
From the University of Wisconsin Extension, providing information about distance education and its delivery

www.outreach.psu.edu/users/atb/main.htm
Pennsylvania State University
Electronic library and links to distance education research sites

ericir.syr.edu/
AskERIC
Educational Resources Information Center Federally funded national information system that provides information on all aspects of education to teachers

illinois.online.uillinois.edu
Comprehensive Distance Education List of Resources
Links to distance education Web sites compiled by Illinois On-Line Network at the University of Illinois

www.searchedu.com
Over 20 million **international university and education pages** indexed and categorized

www.uidaho.edu/evo/distglan.html
Online series of papers, reports, and explanations **about distance learning**

www.nces.ed.gov/ipeds/cool/Search.asp
National Center for Educational Statistics

www.powerstudents.com
Information **about higher education**

www.ed.gov
U.S. Department of Education

www.nces.ed.gov
U.S. Department of Education's National Center for Education Statistics

Distance Learning Technology:

www.videoconference.com
Videoconferencing information

www.kn.pacbell.com/wired/vidconf/home.html
Videoconferencing for learning

www.netskills.ac.uk
Online interactive self-paced **tutorial** on the Web to help those new to the Internet

www.pcwebopedia.com
Online dictionary of Internet and computer-related terms

www.ask.com
Ask Jeeves
Great search engine tool

www.google.com
Google
Great search engine tool

Examination Programs:

www.acenet.edu
American Council on Education
Center for Adult Learning and Educational Credentials

www.cael.org
Council for Adult and Experiential Learning (CAEL)

www.collegeboard.org/clep
College Entrance Examination Board
CLEP enables you to obtain college credit by testing for knowledge you already possess.

www.ets.org
Educational Testing Service (ETS)
This organization administers the GRE and other testing programs.

www.toefl.org
Test of English as a Foreign Language (TOEFL)
English-proficiency testing services for international students

www.review.com
Princeton Review standardized **test preparation services**

Financial Resources for Scholarships and Financial Aid:

www.embark.com
Embark
Apply online to the school of your choice and discover which schools will offer you financial aid.

www.finaid.org
Distance Learning Calculator

www.ed.gov/offices/OSFAP/Students
U.S. Department of Education financial aid section

www.collegeboard.org/finaid/fastud/
html/efc.html
The College Board's EFC calculator

www.ed.gov/prog_info/SFA/StudentGuide/
2000-1/need.html
U.S. Department of Education section about he EFC

www.finaid.org/calculators/
finaidestimate.phtml
Finaid's EFC calculator

easi.ed.gov/studentcenter/html/
applylstate.html
Listing of state grant and state guaranty agencies

www.finaid.org/otheraid/tax.phtml
Finaid's section on **tax credits**

www.fafsa.ed.gov
Free Application for Financial Student Aid (FAFSA)
Filling out this form allows you to find out your EFC.

www.students.gov/states.cfm
Information on **state grants** for students

apps.collegeboard.com/fincalc/efc_
welcome.jsp
CSS/Financial Aid Profile
Financial aid program administered by the College Board

www.meritmoney.com
Merit Money
The only existing searchable database of academic scholarships available from colleges and universities

www.fastweb.com
Fast Web
The largest searchable database of private and corporate scholarships

www.collegeboard.org/fundfinder/
html/ssrchtop.html
College Board Scholarship
Scholarship search engine

www.ed.gov/offices/OFSFAP/Students/
taxcuts/credits.html
Educational tax credit info

Finding Jobs and Internships:

www.internshipprograms.com
Searchable database of internship opportunities

www.studentadvantage.com
Contains many articles written by students on **topics related to internship programs**

www.jobmonkey.com
Find unique opportunities to **travel the world**, have fun, and earn money doing it

Help for College-Level Writing and Research:

www.back2college.com/essay1.htm
Application essay advice

www.collegeexpress.com/admissions/essay.html
Application essay advice

www.bartleby.com/141/index.html
William Strunk Jr.'s Elements of Style

owl.english.purdue.edu/
Online Writing Lab at Purdue University

departments.colgate.edu/diw/NWCAOWLS.html
Online writing lab

webster.commnet.edu/apa/apa_intro.htm
webster.commnet.edu/mla.htm
APA and MLA style
The unofficial guide to APA and MLA styles

www.loc.gov
The Library of Congress

www.bibliomania.com
Full texts of **classic fiction online**

etext.lib.virginia.edu
University of Virginia Library

www.bartleby.com/99
A **collection of passages**, phrases, and proverbs traced to their sources in ancient and modern literature

Non-credit Courses—Training Providers:

www.click2learn.com
Click2Learn
Computer, management, and entrepreneurial skills training

www.learn2.com
Learn2.com
Online training company that offers course outlines for review

www.nationalcollegeonline.com
National College
Online training company

www.thinq.com
THINQ
Business and technology courses from many providers

www.youachieve.com
youachieve.com
Online training company that offers 372 different online classes

www.universityaccess.com
University Access
Online business school that offers classes in business communications, macroeconomics, marketing, and entrepreneurship

Study Resources:

sunsite.berkeley.edu
Berkeley Digital Library
Text and image collections, search tools, databases, and lists of teaching and training resources

www.Britannica.com
Britannica Online
Up-to-date news stories, magazines, and books to browse, as well as a Merriam Webster Dictionary and the entire Encyclopedia Britannica online

www.infoplease.com
Information Please
Research links, databases, tools, almanacs, history information, biographies, and current-events stories

www.researchpaper.com
ResearchPaper.com
Tips and tools for researching online and the capability of searching by research topic

www.newsdirectory.com/college_news.php
Links to **college newspaper** Web sites

scholar.google.com
Scholarly Journals on the Web
Directory of scholarly and research-oriented journals

www.lib.uwaterloo.ca/society/webpages.html
Scholarly Societies on the Web
Listing of over 1,400 online scholarly societies

www.lsoft.com/lists/listref.html
Listservs
Searchable, complete, up-to-date database of over **42,000 listservs**

firstsearch.oclc.org
First Search
Worldwide library search engine site

www.iln.net
Interactive Learning Network
Online tutoring, subject lessons, video lectures, and handy subject reviews

www.hungryminds.com
Hungry Minds
Contains separate pages for individual academic subjects

www.biology.arizona.edu
University of Arizona Biology Site

Appendix F:
Accrediting Agencies*

Regional

Middle States Association of Colleges and Schools (MSA)
Middle States Commission on Higher Education
Jean Avnet Morse, Executive Director
3624 Market Street, 2nd Floor Annex
Philadelphia, PA 19104
Phone: (267) 284-5000
Fax: (215) 662-5950
E-mail: info@msche.org
Web: www.msche.org
States: Delaware, District of Columbia, Maryland, New Jersey, New York, Pennsylvania, Puerto Rico, Virgin Islands

New England Association of Schools and Colleges (NEASC-CIHE)
Commission on Institutions of Higher Education
Barbara Brittingham, Director
209 Burlington Road
Bedford, MA 01730
Phone: (781) 271-0022
Fax: (781) 271-0950
E-mail: CIHE@neasc.org
Web: www.neasc.org
States: Connecticut, Maine, Massachusetts, New Hampshire, Rhode Island, Vermont

New England Association of Schools and Colleges (NEASC-CTCI)
Commission on Technical and Career Institutions
Paul Bento, Director
William C. Warren, Associate Director
209 Burlington Road
Bedford, MA 01730
Phone: (781) 271-0022
Fax: (781) 271-0950
E-mail: pbento@neasc.org
E-mail: wwarren@neasc.org
Web: www.neasc.org

North Central Association of Colleges and Schools (NCA-HLC)
The Higher Learning Commission
Steven D. Crow, Executive Director
30 North LaSalle, Suite 2400
Chicago, IL 60602
Phone: (312) 263-0456
Fax: (312) 263-7462
E-mail: info@hlcommission.org
Web: www.ncahigherlearningcommission.org
States: Arizona, Arkansas, Colorado, Illinois, Indiana, Iowa, Kansas, Michigan, Minnesota, Missouri, Nebraska, New Mexico, North Dakota, Ohio, Oklahoma, South Dakota, West Virginia, Wisconsin, Wyoming

*Updated information is available at www.chea.org and www.ed.gov

Northwest Commission on Colleges and Universities (NWCCU)
Sandra E. Elman, President
8060 165th Avenue, NE, Suite 100
Redmond, WA 98052
Phone: (425) 558-4224
Fax: (425) 376-0596
E-mail: selman@nwccu.org
Web: www.nwccu.org
States: Alaska, Idaho, Montana, Nevada, Oregon, Utah, Washington

Southern Association of Colleges and Schools (SACS)
Commission on Colleges
Belle S. Wheelan, President
1866 Southern Lane
Decatur, GA 30033
Phone: (404) 679-4500
Fax: (404) 679-4558
E-mail: bwheelan@sacscoc.org
Web: www.sacs.org
States: Alabama, Florida, Georgia, Kentucky, Louisiana, Mississippi, North Carolina, South Carolina, Tennessee, Texas, Virginia

Western Association of Schools and Colleges (WASC-ACCJC)
Accrediting Commission for Community and Junior Colleges
Barbara A. Beno, President
10 Commercial Boulevard, Suite 204
Novato, CA 94949
Phone: (415) 506-0234
Fax: (415) 506-0238
E-mail: accjc@accjc.org
Web: www.accjc.org

Western Association of Schools and Colleges (WASC-ACSCU)
Accrediting Commission for Senior Colleges and Universities
Ralph A. Wolff, Executive Director
985 Atlantic Avenue, Suite 100
Alameda, CA 94501
Phone: (510) 748-9001
Fax: (510) 748-9797
E-mail: wascsr@wascsenior.org
Web: www.wascweb.org
States: remaining states not covered previously

U.S. Department of Education
Division of Eligibility and Agency Evaluation
Bureau of Postsecondary Education
400 Maryland Avenue, SW
Washington, DC 20202-0498
1-800-USA-LEARN (1-800-872-5327)
www.ed.gov

The Council For Higher Education Accreditation
Council For Higher Education Accreditation (CHEA)
One Dupont Circle NW, Suite 510
Washington DC, 20036-1135
Phone: (202) 955-6126
Fax: (202) 955-6129
Web: www.ed.gov

Accrediting Commission of the Distance Education and Training Council (DETC)
Michael P. Lambert, Executive Director
1601 Eighteenth Street NW, Suite 2
Washington, DC 20009
Phone: (202) 234-5100
Fax: (202) 332-1386
E-mail: detc@detc.org
Web: www.detc.org

Faith Based

Association for Biblical Higher Education
Commission on Accreditation
Formerly the Accrediting Association of Bible
Colleges (AABC)
Larry McKinney, Executive Director
5575 South Semoran Boulevard, Suite 26
Orlando, FL 32822
Phone: (407)207-0808
Fax: (407) 207-0840
E-mail: info@abhe.org
Web: www.abhe.org

Association of Advanced Rabbinical and
Talmudic Schools (AARTS)
Bernard Fryshman, Executive Vice President
11 Broadway, Suite 405
New York, NY 10004
Phone: (212)363-1991
Fax: (212)533-5335

Commission on Accrediting of the
Association of Theological Schools in the
United States and Canada (ATS)
Daniel O. Aleshire, Executive Director
10 Summit Park Drive
Pittsburgh, PA 15275
Phone: (412) 788-6505
Fax: (412) 788-6510
E-mail: ats@ats.edu
Web: www.ats.edu

Transnational Association of Christian
Colleges and Schools (TRACS)
Accreditation Commission
Russell Guy Fitzgerald, Executive Director
15935 Forest Road, PO Box 328
Forest, VA 24551
Phone: (434) 525-9539
Fax: (434) 525-9538
E-mail: info@tracs.org
Web: www.tracs.org

Association for Clinical Pastoral
Education, Inc.
Accreditation Commission
Teresa E. Snorton, Executive Director
1549 Claremont Road, Suite 103
Decatur, Georgia 30033-4611
Phone: (404) 320-1472
Fax: (404) 320-0849
E-mail address: acpe@acpe.edu
Web address: www.acpe.edu

Specialized

National Architectural Accrediting
Board
1735 New York Ave. NW
Washington, DC 20006
Phone: (202) 783-2007
Fax: (202) 783-2822
(Recognized by CHEA but not by U.S. Department of Education)

Accrediting Council for Independent
Colleges and Schools (ASICS)
750 First Street NE, Suite 980
Washington, DC 20002
Phone: (202) 336-6780

Fax: (202) 482-2593
Web: www.asics.org

Association of Collegiate Business Schools and Programs
7007 College Blvd., Suite 420
Overland Park, KS 66211
Phone: (913) 339-9356
Fax: (913) 339-6226
E-mail: info@acbsp.org
Web: www.acbsp.org
(Recognized by CHEA but not by U.S. Department of Education)

Accrediting Council for Continuing Education and Training
1722 N Street, N.W.
Washington, D.C. 20036
Phone: (202) 955-1113
FAX: (202) 955-1118
Web: www.accet.org

Distance Education and Training Council
1601 18th Street NW
Washington, DC 20009
Phone: (202) 234-5100
Fax: (202) 332-1386
Web: www.detc.org

American Academy for Liberal Education
1050 17th Street, NW, Suite 400
Washington, DC 20036
Phone: (202) 452-8611
Fax: (202) 452-8620

Montessori Accreditation Council for Teacher Education, Commission on Accreditation
524 Main Street, Suite 202
Racine, WI 53403
Phone: (262) 898-1846
Fax: (262) 898-1849
Web: www.MACTE.org

Council on Occupational Education
41 Perimeter Center East, NE, Suite 640
Atlanta, GA 30346
Phone: (800) 917-2081
Fax: (770) 396-3790

American Bar Association
321 North Clark Street, 21st Floor
Chicago, Illinois 60610-4714
Phone: (312) 988-6746,
Fax (312) 988-5681
E-mail: sebertj@staff.abanet.org
Web: www.abanet.org/legaled/

Accrediting Bureau of Health Education Schools
2700 South Quincy Street
Suite 210
Arlington, VA 22206
Phone: (703) 998-1200
Fax: (703) 998-2550
Accredits programs for Medical Laboratory Technician and Medical Assistant

American Dental Association
211 East Chicago Ave., 18th Floor
Chicago, IL 60611
Phone: (312) 440-2500
Fax: (312) 440-2915
E-mail: prebled@ada.org
Web: www.ada.org

Council on Naturopathic Medical Education
P.O. Box 178
Great Barrington, Massachusetts 01230
Phone: (413) 528-8877
Fax: (413) 528-8880
E-mail: council@cnme.org
Web: www.cnme.org

Midwifery Education Accreditation Board
20 E. Cherry Avenue
Flagstaff, Arizona 86001-4607
Phone: (928) 214-0997
Fax: (928) 773-9694
E-mail: info@meacschools.org
Web: www.meacschools.org

Commission on Opticianry Accreditation
8665 Sudley Road, #341
Manassas, Virginia 20110-4588
Phone: (703) 940-9134
Fax: (703) 940-9135
E-mail: coa@coaccreditation.com
Web: www.coaccreditation.com

American Council on Pharmaceutical Education
20 North Clark Street, Suite 2500
Chicago, Illinois 60602-5109
Phone: (312) 664-3575
Fax: (312) 664-46522
E-mail: pvlasses@acpe-accredit.org
Web: www.acpe-accredit.org

Council on Education for Public Health
800 St. NW Suite 202
Washington, DC 20001
Phone: (202) 789-1050
Fax: (202) 789-1895

Joint Review Committee on Education in Radiologic Technology
Joanne S. Greathouse, Executive Director
20 North Wacker Drive, Suite 2850
Chicago, Illinois 60606-3182
Phone: (312) 704-5300
Fax: (312) 704-5304
E-mail: mail@jrcert.org
Web: www.jrcert.org

National Environmental Health Science & Protection Accreditation Council
National Environmental Health Association
720 S. Colorado Blvd. Ste. 970-S
Denver, CO 80246-1925
Phone: (303) 756-9090
e-mail: staff@neha.org

National Association of Industrial Technology
3300 Washtenaw Ave., Suite 220
Ann Arbor, MI 48104
Phone: (734) 677-0720
(Recognized by CHEA but not by U.S. Department of Education)

American Academy of Microbiology
1725 N. St. NW
Washington, DC 20036
Phone: (202) 942-9225
Fax: (202) 942-6932
(Recognized by CHEA but not by U.S. Department of Education)

National Accrediting Commission of Cosmetology Arts and Sciences

4401 Ford Avenue, Suite 1300
Arlington, Virginia 22303
Phone: (703) 600-7600
Fax: (703) 379-2200
E-mail: cwalck@naccas.org
Web: www.naccas.org

New York State Board of Regents
State Education Department, Education Building

Albany, NY 12234
Phone: (518) 474-3852
Web: www.nysed.gov/regents/

Commission on Collegiate Nursing Education (CCNE)

One Dupont Circle, NW, Suite 530
Washington, DC 20036
Phone: (202) 887-6791
Fax: (202) 887-8476
E-mail: jbutlin@aacn.nche.edu
Web: www.aacn.nche.edu/accreditation

Council on Aviation Accreditation (CAA)
Aviation Accreditation Board International

Gary W. Kiteley, Executive Director
3410 Skyway Drive
Auburn, AL 36830
Phone: (334) 844-2431
Fax: (334) 844-2432
E-mail: caa@auburn.edu
Web: www.aabi.aero.org

Professional

Accreditation Board for Engineering and Technology (ABET)

George D. Peterson, Executive Director
111 Market Place, Suite 1050
Baltimore, MD 21202
Phone: (410) 347-7700
Fax: (410) 625-2238
E-mail: info@abet.org
Web: www.abet.org

Accrediting Commission for Acupuncture and Oriental Medicine

Dort S. Bigg, Executive Director
Maryland Tradecenter 3
7501 Greenway Center Dr., Suite 820
Greenbelt, MD 20770
Phone: (301) 313-0855
Fax: (301) 313-0912
E-mail: acaom1@compuserve.com
Web: www.acaom.org

Accrediting Council on Education in Journalism and Mass Communications

Susanne Shaw, Executive Director
School of Journalism
Stauffer-Flint Hall
1435 Jayhawk Boulevard
University of Kansas
Lawrence, KS 66045
Phone: (785) 864-3986
Fax: (785) 864-5225
E-mail: sshaw@ku.edu
Web: www.ku.edu/~acejmc

American Association for Marriage and Family Therapy (AAMFT/COAMFTE) Commission on Accreditation for Marriage and Family Therapy Education

Jeff S. Harmon, Director of Accreditation
112 South Alfred Street
Alexandria, VA 22314
Phone: (703) 838-9808 (main)
Phone: (703) 253-0457 (direct)
Fax: (703) 253-0508
Email: coamfte@aamft.org
Web: www.aamft.org

American Association of Family and Consumer Sciences (AAFCS) Council for Accreditation (CFA)

Karen Tucker Thomas, Executive Director
1555 King Street
Alexandria, VA 22314
Phone: (703) 706-4600
Fax: (703)706-4663
E-mail: accreditation@aafcs.org
Web: www.aafcs.org

American Association of Nurse Anesthetists Council on Accreditation of Nurse Anesthesia Educational Programs

Francis R. Gerbasi, Executive Director
222 South Prospect Avenue, Suite 304
Park Ridge, IL 60068
Phone: (847) 692-7050 ext. 1154
Fax: (847) 692-7137
E-mail: fgerbasi@aana.com
Web: www.aana.com

American Board of Funeral Service Education (ABFSE) Committee on Accreditation

3432 Ashland Avenue, Suite U
St. Joseph, MO 64506
Phone: (816) 233-3747
Fax: (816) 233-3793
E-mail: exdir@abfse.org
Web: www.abfse.org

American Council for Construction Education (ACCE)

Michael Holland, Executive Vice President
1717 North Loop 1604 East, Suite 320
San Antonio, TX 78232
Phone: (210) 495-6161
Fax: (210) 495-6168
E-mail: acce@acce-hq.org
Web: www.acce-hq.org

American Culinary Federation, Inc. Accrediting Commission

Dawn Jantsch, Managing Director
Roxanne J. Jordan, Director of Education, Accreditation
180 Center Place Way
St. Augustine, FL 32095
Phone: (904) 824-4468
Fax: (904) 825-4758
E-mail: rjordan@acfchefs.net
Web: www.acfchefs.org

American Dietetic Association Commission on Accreditation for Dietetics Education (CADE-ADA)

Beverly E. Mitchell, Executive Director
120 South Riverside Plaza, Suite 2000
Chicago, IL 60606
Phone: (312) 899-4872
Fax: (312) 899-4817
E-mail: bmitchell@eatright.org
Web: www.eatright.org/cade

American Library Association (ALA)Committee on Accreditation

Ann O'Neill, Director, Office for Accreditation
50 East Huron Street
Chicago, IL 60611
Phone: (800) 545-2433
Fax: (312) 280-2433
E-mail: aoneill@ala.org
Web: www.ala.org/accreditation.html

American Occupational Therapy Association (AOTA)
Accreditation Council for Occupational Therapy Education (ACOTE)

Sue Graves, Sr. Program Accreditation Admin.
4720 Montgomery Lane
P.O. Box 31220
Bethesda, MD 20824-1220
Phone: (301)-652-2682
Fax: (301)-652-7711
E-mail: sgraves@aota.org
Web: www.aota.org

American Optometric Association Council on Optometric Education

Joyce Urbeck, Administrative Director
243 North Lindbergh Blvd.
St. Louis, MO 63141
Phone: (314) 991-4100
Fax: (314) 991-4101
E-mail: jlurbeck@theaoa.org
Web: www.aoanet.org

American Osteopathic Association Bureau of Professional Education

Konrad C. Miskowicz-Retz, Director
Department of Education
142 East Ontario Street
Chicago, IL 60611-2864
Phone: (312) 202-8048
Fax: (312) 202-8202
E-mail: kretz@aoa-net.org
Web: www.aoa-net.org

American Podiatric Medical Association Council on Podiatric Medical Education (CPME)

Alan Tinkleman, Director
9312 Old Georgetown Road
Bethesda, MD 20814-1698
Phone: (301) 571-9200
Fax: (301) 571-4903
E-mail: artinkleman@apma.org
Web: www.cpme.org

American Psychological Association (APA)
Committee on Accreditation
Susan Zlotlow, Director
Office of Program Consultation
and Accreditation
750 First Street, NE
Washington, DC 20002-4242
Phone: (202) 336-5979
Fax: (202) 336-5978
E-mail: szlotlow@apa.org
Web: www.apa.org

American Society of Landscape Architects (ASLA) Landscape Architectural Accreditation Board
Ronald C. Leighton, Accreditation Manager
636 I Street, NW
Washington, DC 20001-3736
Phone: (202) 898-2444
Fax: (202) 898-1185
E-mail: rleighton@asla.org
Web: www.asla.org

American Speech-Language-Hearing Association (ASHA)
Council on Academic Accreditation in Audiology and Speech-Language Pathology
Patrima Tice, Director of Credentialing
10801 Rockville Pike
Rockville, MD 20852
Phone: (301) 897-5700
Fax: (301) 571-0457
E-mail: ptice@asha.org
Web: www.asha.org

American Veterinary Medical Association
Division of Education and Research
Don G. Simmons
Director of Education and Research
1931 North Meacham Road, Suite 100
Schaumburg, IL 60173-4360
Phone: (847) 925-8070 ext. 236
Fax: (847) 925-1329
E-mail: dsimmons@avma.org
Web: www.avma.org

Association of American Law Schools (AALS)
Carl Monk, Executive Director
1201 Connecticut Avenue NW, Suite 800
Washington, DC 20036-2605
Phone: (202) 296-8851
Fax: (202) 296-8869
E-mail: cmonk@aals.org
Web: www.aals.org

Commission on Accreditation in Physical Therapy Education
American Physical Therapy Association
Mary Jane Harris, Director
1111 North Fairfax Street
Alexandria, VA 22314
Phone: (703) 706-3245
Fax: (703) 838-8910
E-mail: maryjaneharris@apta.org
Web: www.apta.org

Commission on Accreditation of Allied Health Education Programs (CAAHEP)
Kathleen Megivern, Executive Director
1361 Park Street
Clearwater, FL 33756
Phone: (727) 210-2350
Fax: (727) 210-2354
E-mail: mail@caahep.org
Web: www.caahep.org

Computer Science Accreditation Commission (CSAC) of the Computing Sciences Accreditation Board (CSAB)
Merged with Accreditation Board for Engineering and Technology, Inc. (ABET), September 30, 2001

Council for Accreditation of Counseling and Related Educational Programs
American Counseling Association

Carol L. Bobby, Executive Director
5999 Stevenson Avenue
Alexandria, VA 22304
Phone: (703) 823-9800 ext. 301
Fax: (703) 823-1581
E-mail: cacrep@cacrep.org
Web: www.cacrep.org

Council on Chiropractic Education
Commission on Accreditation
Martha S. O'Connor, Executive Vice President
8049 N. 85th Way
Scottsdale, Arizona 85258-4321
Phone: (480) 443-8877
Fax (480) 483-7333
E-mail: cce@cce-usa.org
Web: www.cce-usa.org

Council on Rehabilitation Education
Commission on Standards and Accreditation

Marvin D. Kuehn, Executive Director
1835 Rohlwing Road, Suite E
Rolling Meadows, IL 60008
Phone: (847) 394-1785
Fax: (847) 394-2108
E-mail: kuehnmar@emporia.edu
Web: www.core-rehab.org

Council on Social Work Education
Division of Standards and Accreditation
Dean Pierce, Director
1725 Duke Street, Suite 500
Alexandria, VA 22314
Phone: (703) 683-8080
Fax: (703) 739-9048
E-mail: dpierce@cswe.org
Web: www.cswe.org

Foundation for Interior Design Accreditation
Kayem Dunn, Executive Director
146 Monroe Center, NW, Suite 1318
Grand Rapids, MI 49503-2920
Phone: (616) 458-0400
Fax: (616) 458-0460
E-mail: info@accredit-id.org
Web: www.accredit-id.org

Joint Review Committee on Educational Programs in Nuclear Medicine Technology (JRCNMT)
Elaine Cuklanz, Executive Director
716 Black Point Road
P.O. Box 1149
Polson, Montana 59860-1149
Phone: (406) 883-0003
Fax: (406) 883-0022
E-mail: rcnmt@centurytel.net
Web: www.jrcnmt.org

Liaison Committee on Medical Education (LCME)

In even-numbered years beginning July 1, contact:
Carol A. Aschenbrener, Secretary
AAMC Secretary to the LCME
Vice President, Medical School Standards &
Assessment
Association of American Medical Colleges
2450 N Street, NW
Washington, DC 20037
Phone: (202) 828-0596
Fax: (202) 828-1125
E-mail: caschenbrener@aamc.org
Web: www.lcme.org

In odd-numbered years beginning July 1, contact:
Frank A. Simon, M.D.
AMA Secretary to the LCME
Assistant Vice President, Medical Education
American Medical Association
515 North State Street
Chicago, IL 60610
Phone: (312) 464-4657
Fax: (312) 464-5830
E-mail: frank_simon@ama-assn.org
Web: www.lcme.org

National Accrediting Agency for Clinical Laboratory Sciences (NAACLS)

Olive M. Kimball, Executive Director
8410 West Bryn Mawr Avenue, Suite 670
Chicago, IL 60631
Phone: (773) 714-8880
Fax: (773) 714-8886
E-mail: info@naacls.org
Web: naacls.org

National Association of Schools of Art and Design (NASAD)

Samuel Hope, Executive Director
Karen P. Moynahan, Associate Director
11250 Roger Bacon Drive, Suite 21
Reston, VA 20190
Phone: (703) 437-0700
Fax: (703) 437-6312
E-mail: info@arts-accredit.org
Web: www.arts-accredit.org

National Association of Schools of Dance

Samuel Hope, Executive Director
Karen P. Moynahan, Associate Director
11250 Roger Bacon Drive, Suite 21
Reston, VA 20190
Phone: (703) 437-0700
Fax: (703) 437-6312
E-mail: info@arts-accredit.org
Web: www.arts-accredit.org

National Association of Schools of Theatre

11250 Roger Bacon Drive. Suite 21
Reston, Virginia 20190
Phone: (703) 437-0700
Fax (703) 437-6312
E-mail: info@arts-accredit.org
Web: www.arts-accredit.org

National Association of Schools of Music

Samuel Hope, Executive Director
Karen P. Moynahan, Associate Director
11250 Roger Bacon Drive, Suite 21
Reston, VA 20190
Phone: (703) 437-0700
Fax (703) 437-6312
E-mail: info@arts-accredit.org
Web: www.arts-accredit.org

National Association of Schools of Public Affairs and Administration (NASPAA) Commission on Peer Review and Accreditation (CORPRA)

Jinla Byrne, Director of Accreditation

1120 G Street, NW, Suite 730

Washington, DC 20005

Phone: (202)628-8965

Fax: (202)626-4978

E-mail: naspaa@naspaa.org

Web: www.naspaa.org

National League for Nursing Accrediting Commission, Inc. (NLNAC)

Patricia R. Forni, Executive Director

61 Broadway

New York, NY 10006

Phone: (800) 669-1656 ext. 153

Phone: (212) 363-5555 ext. 153

Fax: (212) 812-0390

E-mail: pforni@nlnac.org

Web: www.nlnac.org

National Recreation & Park Association/ American Association for Physical Activity and Recreation (NRPA/AAPAR) Council on Accreditation

Danielle Timmerman,

Academic Affairs Manager

22377 Belmont Ridge Road

Ashburn, VA 20148

Phone: (703) 858-2150

Fax: (703) 858-0794

E-mail: dtimmerman@nrpa.org

Web: www.councilonaccreditation.org

Society of American Foresters (SAF)

Terrance A. Clark, Associate Director of Science & Education

5400 Grosvenor Lane

Bethesda, MD 20814

Phone: (301) 897-8720 ext. 123

Fax: (301) 897-3690

E-mail: clarkt@safnet.org

Web: www.safnet.org

Teacher Education Accreditation Council, Accreditation Committee

Frank B. Murray, President

One Dupont Circle, Suite 320

Washington, DC 20036-0110

Phone: (202) 466-7236

Fax (202) 466-7238

E-mail address: frank@teac.org

Web address: www.teac.org

Index

A

academic discussion, 66
Accelerated Distance Learners Guide To Colleges, 153
accelerated
  learner, 93
  learning techniques, 15, 21, 104
  reading, 97
  study, 132
  test taking, 131
  writing, 121
Accreditation Board for Engineering and Technology, 144
accreditation, 144-145
accredited
  degree, 14, 18
  school, 143
active reading, 104
Adams, John, 131
Advanced Placement (AP), 31
advising center, 151
advisors, 60, 62, 150, 175-176
aesthetic dimensions, 180
American Psychological Association (APA), 122, 129
analogies, 105
annotated bibliography, 42, 44
answering questions, 134
Application for Financial Student Aid (AFSA), 158
area concentration, 178
areas of learning, 38
Aristotle, 108
Asian Development Studies, 29
Ask Jeeves, 80

assignments, 57, 65
  proofreading, 126
  structuring for flexibility, 71
association list, 109, 111-112
asynchronous communication, 62
audio classes, 63
audioconference, 64
audio-visual materials, 59
auditory learner, 108, 109, 119
Aviation Science, 29
awards, 42

B

bachelor of arts, 178, 182
bachelor's degree, 15, 74, 175, 178
background checks, 143
backskipping, 99
baroque music, 118
Berg, Howard Stephen, 97, 102
Berkeley Digital Library Sunsite, 84
Berlin, Irving, 173
Beroth, David, 73
Bible, 192
Bonaparte, Napolean, 15
Bonstrom, Erik, 184
brain, 93, 97, 112, 118
  capacities of, 114
  design of, 114
  potential of, 107
breathing, 133
Brigham Young University, 166
Britannica Online, 84
broadcasts, live, 63
budgets, 76

Bulgaria, 118
bulletin boards, electronic, 66
Business Administration, 14, 178
Business Ethics, 163

C

Caasi, Heidi, 46
calendar, 81
California State University, 166
camera, 98
Campus Books, 85
CD-ROM, 65
Center for Independent Learning, 76
chains
  storing information in, 109
  thinking in, 109
Charter Oak State College, 22, 45, 150, 152, 180
chat session, 66
CHEA, 144
Chesterfield, Lord, 171
China, 14, 36, 119, 195
Christian education, 149
chunking, 111
Churchill, Winston, 95
classical music, 118
classrooms, 6, 36, 61
CLEP, 22, 23, 73, 155, 156
College Board, The, 31, 132, 159
college
  budget sheet, 161
  catalogs, 39, 152, 174
  catalogs, online, 39
  choosing a, 143, 152

credit, 29
  enrolling in, 22
  expenses, 157
  finding a, 81
  libraries, 39
  money required for, 184
  papers, 121
  staff, 62
  technical, 73
  traditional, 14, 155
  transcript, 46
  tuition, 156, 158
  Web sites, 81
color, 114, 116
communication, 61, 170
  skills, 70
communications technology,
  62, 76
community college, 72, 73
community residents, 74
comprehension, 97, 99, 103
computer, 60, 165, 170
computer-testing lab, 58
concentration, 118, 133, 179
  maximum, 105
  powers of, 14
connections, making, 116
consulting, 14
contextual clues, 102
continuing education, 47
Cope, Andrew, 56
correspondence courses, 14,
  29, 55, 175
correspondence study, 147
costs, calculating, 75
Council for Higher Education,
  144
course, 74
  catalogs, 38, 81, 178
  choosing a, 55
  community college, 75
  descriptions on the web, 39

descriptions, 38, 41
extension fee, 59
general education, 73
high-school, 21
independent study, 76
mapping a, 174
online, 58, 174
planning, 163
prerequisites, 58
registration, 60, 176
required, 21
requirements, 58
selection, 152
specialized, 168
syllabus, 38, 81, 121
traditional, 77, 176
creative association, 112
creative links, 116
creative memorization, 111
credential evaluation fee, 59
credentials, 48, 73
credit, 175
  banking, 22
  earning through multiple
    institutions, 152
  earning, 21, 26, 30, 43
  equivalency, 51
  life experience, 38
  lower-level, 30, 178
  transfer fee, 59
  transferring, 56
  upper-level, 30, 178
credit-by-examination, 21, 22,
29, 156, 179
cum laude, 30
customized learning, 9, 36, 70
cybercasts, 65

D ————————————
Dahl, Ingrid, 149
DANTES Subject Standardized
  Tests, 26

Degree, 155
  audits, 168
  programs, 38, 55, 175
  requirements, 23, 175
  specialization, 69
degree-completion schedule,
  174
degree-completion worksheet,
  179
descriptive essay, 123
DETC, 145
diet, 169
diploma, 42, 143
discouragement, 100
discussion groups, 81
distance learning, 17, 36
  courses, 61, 121, 122
  methods, 15
  opportunities, 102
  programs, 81
distractions, eliminating, 98
divided memory, 112
documentation, 36, 56, 122
double speed drill, 99
DSL, 86
DSSTS, 26

E ————————————
Edison, Thomas, 107
education, 6, 90, 94
  alternative methods of, 75
  new paradigm of, 184
  online, 55
  up-to-date, 36
EFC, 158, 162
efficiency, 93, 163, 164, 166,
  168, 169
Einstein, Albert, 36, 94, 98, 110
Embark, 81
English Composition test, 23
English, 178
enrollment, 24, 149

schedule, 149
entrepreneurs, 195
essay, 123, 124, 145
   answers, 133
   exams, 136
   questions, 133
   short, 31
examination
   answers, 135
   directions, 134
   guides, 22
   minimum score, 21
   proctoring, 74
   program, college level, 23
Excelsior College
   Examinations (ECE), 25
Excelsior College, 22, 152, 182
exercise, 133, 169
Expected Family Contribution
(EFC), 158
expenses, 157
experience, 18, 36, 43

F ——————————————

faculty members, 72
FAFSA, 158
file cabinet, 109, 167
financial aid, 145, 157
   planning, 156
   profile, 159
First Search, 83
flashing, 117
focus, 98, 99, 101
foreign language, 31, 118, 119
free electives, 178

G ——————————————

genius, 12, 97, 118
German, 110
Gettysburg Address, 110
global economy, 51

Global Leadership Institute,
   15, 195
Global Learning Strategies, 195
goals, 15, 71, 174, 180
Goodwin, Jim, 15
Google, 80
GPA, 174
Gracian, Baltasar, 57
Graduate Record Exams
   (GRE), 32
graduate school, 143, 174, 182
grants, 155, 156, 159, 173
graphics, 65
Greggs Reference Manual,
   The, 122
guessing techniques, 134
Guide Book, 89, 189
guided study, 69
guiding finger motion, 99
Guinness Book of World
   Records, 97

H ——————————————

Harvard, 143, 155
Haydn, Joseph, 118
health-care-related subjects,
   25
help line, 151
Herbster, Robert D., 151
home-study program, 166
Hubbard, Elbert, 164
Human Resources
   Management, 168
Hungry Minds, 84
hypertext, 63

I ——————————————

Illingworth, Ronald D., 64
import/export business, 70
independent learning, 94, 147,
   168

independent studies, 14, 70,
   149
Indiana University, 56
instruction,
   audio, 58
   multimedia, 147
   quality and type of, 65, 143
instructional phase, 21
instructional tools, web based,
   58
instructors, 17, 64
Interactive Learning Network,
   84
interactive learning, 65
interlibrary loan service, 83
intern, 13
International
   Business Ethics, 36
   Economics, 14
   Management, 14
Internet, 62, 74, 76, 86
   filtering, 79
   traffic, 79
internships, 47, 49, 182
   academic worth of, 51
   college credit for, 51
   existing program, 48
   opportunities for, 47
   self-made, 48
Internship Search Engine, 52
Internshipprograms.com, 52
investments, 106

J ——————————————

Jackson, Holbrook, 97
job market, 192
Job Monkey, 53
junior college, 72

K

Kettering, Charles, 5
keyword, 116, 136, 137
   notes, 124
kinesthetic learner, 108, 109, 119
knowledge-based economy, 192

L

lab equipment, specialized, 64
Landers, Ann, 132
languages, 31
laziness, 171
leaders, 7, 195
leadership capacity, 30
learning
   college-level, 38
   computer-assisted, 63
   contract, 48
   experience, quality of, 69, 71
   gateway questions, 94
   groups, 108
   journal, 52
   language, 50
   opportunities, 11, 48
   real-life, 35
   revolution, 102
   skills, accelerated, 173
   strategy, 108
   structuring, 55, 107
   student-directed, 71
   styles, individual, 69
   ten principles of, 7
   text based, 61
   three basic pathways for, 108
learning maps, 103, 104, 114, 121, 124
   constructing a, 114
   example, 115

memorizing, 116
lectures, 61, 63, 64
   recorded, 58
left-brain, 114
legitimate degree programs, 143
liberal arts, 178
libraries, 58, 72, 74, 83, 97, 176
   resources, 163
licenses, 42
licensing exams, 184
life purpose, 173
lifelong learning, 192
Lincoln, Abraham, 110
linear notes, 116
listservs, 82
local residents, 72
long-term memory, consolidating, 117

M

Macroeconomics, 163, 176
major, 145, 146, 174
Martin, Robert, 7
Marx, Groucho, 168
Master Level Reading, 99
master's degrees, 182
mathematical concepts, 103
Mega Learning Corporation, 102
Mega Memory, 119
Mega Speed Reading, 14, 101, 106
Memorization
   rote, 95
   strategies, 117
   techniques, 111, 119
memory,
   building, 90, 101
   long-term, 100, 105, 112
   short-term, 105, 112
mentors, 36, 150

Meritmoney, 159
military, 26, 30
mind's eye, 110, 112, 116
mock test, 133
Modern Language Association (MLA), 122
monthly planner, 165
motivation, 9, 173
multimedia, 58, 65
multiple-choice, 135
multisensory pathway, 119
multitasking, 168
music, 110, 118

N

networking, 36
neural networks, 119
New York State University, 22
New York University Foreign Language Testing Program, 31
nonresident, 58
notes, making, 103, 114, 166
number pictures, 110
numbered lists, 116

O

objective facts, 122
Official CLEP Study Guide, 25
Ohio State University, 22, 29, 152
online application, 146
online courses, 55
on-the-job training, 47
opportunity costs, 155
opportunity, global, 12
organization, 164, 166
organizing references, 128
outlines, 121
   sequential, 114

P ————————

pegging, 112-114
Pell Grant, 162
performance, acedemic, 58
perseverance, 95, 180
personal attention, 70
personal Web pages, 58
perspective, global, 13, 50
Peterson's Internships, 53
Philippines, 13, 31, 36
pictographs, 116
pictures
    storing information as, 108
    using, 109
    viewing, 108
Pinkerton, Dan, 156
Political Science, 182
portfolio, 14, 35, 36, 45, 81,
147, 150, 156, 174
    advisor, 40, 41
    chronological method
      for, 40
    credit, 175
    evaluators, 40
    evidence for, 38
    process, five steps of, 37
    narrative, 38, 40, 41, 51
    worksheet, 42
Principles of
    Management, 168
prior learning, 14
problem-solving,
    collaborative, 66
proctors, 22, 24, 74
professors, 39, 55, 56, 61, 64,
69, 121, 122, 136, 163
    working one-on-one
      with, 70
*Program Planning
    Handbook*, 151
Prometric Testing Centers, 25
Pudewa, Andrew, 129
Purdue University, 128

Q ————————

quarter hours, 29
questions
    effective, 103
    multiple-choice, 133, 135
    test-related, 132
quizzes, short oral, 64

R ————————

reading, 97-98
    comprehension, 103
    drills, 99
    multiple speeds for, 99
references, using, 127, 145
Regents College Examinations
    (RCE), 30
Regents College, 30
registrar, 147
registration deadlines, 60
research, 66, 72, 76, 107, 124
    online, 80, 163
    up-to-date, 81
résumé, 51, 145
retention, levels of, 103
review, 100, 116, 117, 124, 132
revitalizers, 133
right-brain, 114

S ————————

sample exams, 22, 132, 133
savings, 157
schedules, 57, 62, 164, 175
    flexible, 74
Schiesz, Ronald J., 76
Scholarly Societies on the Web,
    82
scholarship, 155, 156, 158, 159,
    173
schools
    finding, 81
    unaccredited, 143
Schwind, David, 30

scientists, 107
search engines, 80
semester hours, 29
semesters, 149
    sixteen-week, 57
Simonides, 112
skimming, 99
sleep, 117, 169
    schedule, 170
Small Business
    Management, 50
sorting information, 109
spatial awareness, 114
specialization, 179
speed, increasing, 97
speed-reading, 90
spreadsheets, 65
standardized examinations,
    42, 145
Stanford University, 156
state college, 58, 156
state grants, 158
strategy, 117
    perfect, 134
stretching, 169
Student Advantage, 53, 85
study, 66
    guides, 22, 166
    independent, 71, 81, 156,
      163, 174
    materials, 83
    mathematical, 110
    part-time, 101
    periods, 105
    resources, 21
    speed, 100
Study Abroad, 81
sugar, 169
summarizing, 104
summary sheet, 132
Swann, Alexandra, 166
syllabus, 39, 40, 42, 61, 81

symbols, 116

synchronous communication, 62

syndromes, avoiding the, 11, 13

synergy, 163, 168

T ————————

Taiwan, 36

teacher's instruction, 63

teaching, 14

    style, 57

TECEP, 27, 28

technology fee, 58

technology, 76

telecommunications charge, 58

telecom*muting*, 5

telephone, 64, 98, 165, 167

television, 98, 168

test

    guide sheets, 132

    prep books, 132

    preparation, 22

    scores, 24

    true or false, 135

Test Administration, Department of, 150

Test Description Book, 28

Testing

    lab, 57, 74

    programs, 21

    rooms, 22

text, viewing, 99

textbooks, 22, 29, 30, 83, 101, 166

Textbooks at Cost, 85

thesis, 123, 124, 136

Thomas Edison College Examination Program (TECEP), 27

Thomas Edison State College, 14, 22, 46, 73, 101, 151, 152, 155, 184

Thoreau, Henry David, 63

to-do list, 98

to-do today, 163, 165

transcripts, 42, 62, 75, 145

    cumulative, 59

transfer credits, 75

Trudeau, Kevin, 109, 119

tuition, 58, 152, 158, 179

    bill, 24, 75

Twain, Mark, 12

Twenty-First-Century Wealth, 156

U ————————

unaccredited, 46

understanding, 36, 37, 170

    developing, 124

university, 74

University of Alaska Fairbanks, 64, 152

V ————————

video, 59, 63, 108, 168

    camera, 108

    instruction, 63

videoconferencing, 58, 63, 65

    desk-top based, 64

    facilities-based, 64

videotapes, 42

violin playing, 118

vision, 50

visual learner, 58, 108, 119

visual pathway, 108, 109

visualization, 104, 112, 115, 137

vocabulary development, 118

    words, 98

Voeller, Bradley, 195

Voeller, David, 180

W ————————

Washington, George, 137

web cams, 65

Whitefield College, 149

Wilde, Oscar, 37

William Jennings Bryan, 13

Wolfgang, Mozart, 118

work experience, 155

work samples, 42

workforce, 35

World Lecture Hall, 81

Write Right Away Writing Technique, 121

writing, 56, 121

    assignment, 121, 122, 124, 129, 168

    cutting and pasting, 127

    excellence in, 129

    experts, 128

    grammar, 126

    labs, online, 128

    legible, 136

    outline form, 122, 124

    persuasive, 122

    power tips for, 129

    projects, 121, 166

    questions, 128

    required layout, 122

    style, 125, 126, 129

    time, 126

Y ————————

Yates, Jared, 182

Yates, Kyle, 101

Student Success Catalog

Dear Friend,

I'm sure that after reading this book you are ready to experience the freedom of distance learning and the time-saving benefits of accelerated learning. Because I have personally gone through the process of using Accelerated Distance Learning to earn my degree, I understand the needs you will have as you work toward the goal of completing your degree. Let me help you! This *Student Success Catalog* is full of the resources you will need to begin your Accelerated Distance Learning.

The information contained in this catalog is probably the most valuable part of the entire book. Here you will find the exact tools you need to be a successful distance learner. Furthermore, because I have personally used each of these resources for my own study, I can assure you they are the very best available. We are constantly adding new products and services, so please visit us at www.globallearningstrategies.org for the most current offerings.

As soon as you are ready to increase the speed and effectiveness of your learning, place your order at **www.globallearningstrategies.org**. We're eager to help you get started!

Your Accelerated Distance Learning friend,
Brad Voeller